"Will The Real Pimps and Hos Please Stand Up!"
Peeping the Multi-leveled Global Game

By
E. Raymond Brown

To Imre, This is all towards the greater conversation. All Game, All Good, All Levels

E. Raymond Brown '04

Copyright © 2002 by E. Burrell

All rights reserved.

No part of this book may be reproduced or transmitted in any form or by any means, electronic or mechanical, including photocopying, recording, or by any information storage or retrieval system, without written permission from Dreamscape Publishing, except for the inclusion of quotations in a review.

Published by Dreamscape Publishing, Inc.
Las Vegas, NV

www.ghettophysics.com

ISBN: 0-9728434-0-X

Text design: Agent Z.
Cover design: Xavier Savant

"The facilitator's task is not to do away with the use of rank and power, but to notice them and make their dynamics explicit for the whole group to see."

A. Mindell

CONTENTS

Introduction
4

Chapter I
I Feel Like I'm Being Pimped!
11

Chapter II
We Create Our Reality: From Metaphysics to Ghettophysics
22

Chapter III
From Whence Cometh This Pimping and Hoing Conversation?
39

The 2003 Ghetto-Famous Pimp Gallery
71

Supporting Pimps
89

Suggested Pimps
95

Keepin' the Pimpin' in Perspective
96

CONTENTS (Cont'd)

Chapter IV
We All Have a Dream, So Give a Pimp and a Ho Room to Grow
98

Chapter V
The Plot Only Gets Thicker
108

Chapter VI
Stand Up, No Matter What!
137

Recommended Reading
178

Acknowledgements
179

Artist's Line-Up
182

About the Author
185

Introduction

Thank God the universe is such an incredibly creative place. Because this book has certainly taken advantage of that and then some! I'm sure it will be useful for the reader to at least have a glimpse of where this whole notion came from. Plus, I know I'm going to be asked about fifty thousand times anyway, so maybe this introduction can help trim that number down.

Well, about two years ago, I was working on a project dealing with the study of archetypes. It was during that time that I became present to the broad dimensionality of the pimp-ho dichotomy. It dawned on me how integral it is in our modern world. But it wasn't until early September 2002 that the whole concept for the book occurred to me.

You know, I honestly don't think that there's anything more raw than paying for, or selling the most intimate bodily act. I mean it's quite a dynamic. You pay, you get down, you go. Yet despite whatever impression the title might create, I am not referring to such a process in this book much at all. What I am using here is the rawness of the dynamic in the one context to relate to the rawness of the social, political and economic dynamics in everyday life.

The fact that many people may not be able to relate on such a level is understandable. It's even a given.

However, I can share with you that this book just came from experience, plain and simple. Sometimes I feel psychologically very groomed and fitted into all this everyday, run-of-the-mill conversation, and its just business as usual. But mostly, I feel very raw. I look out at the world and the things around me, and I see the rawness. I look at global relations and the political state of things, which I am bombarded with information about constantly, and I see a great deal of rawness.

So while I know how to cook up our reality and groom it just for the sake of continuing the daily custom, the fact is I am just not always feeling that. If you really want to know some of what I feel as an American, and more specifically an African-American, then keep turning these pages. Because I can guarantee you one thing – you may or may not be able to relate, but without question, somebody in America will. And you can put that, as my ghetto colleagues say, "on everythang!"

For I'm about to serve this up, "gourmet ghetto intellectual style." Sometimes I will be attempting to carefully carve out a certain type of subtle social dynamic. Yet others, I'm throwing paragraphical flurries like Roy Jones in a bad dream.

I can tell you, the more that I dealt with this subject matter, the more I just had to put things down the way I did, Ebonics and all! I think you'll find the spirit of the project just came right on through me, and it called me into a sort of intensity about it all. ***I must warn you, it's a very confronting conversation, and my only request is that you not blame or get mad with me for how you experience yourself in it.***

What's funny, I have noticed, is that I would not be able to write with any balance toward the two perspectives if I were not in the basic social juxtaposition that I am in. Like many, I have great blessings, yet I'm still struggling my tail off in a real way. Therefore I see both sides of the coin for sure, first hand.

And it's sort of a cool thing. I like the duality of it all. I like the freedom and room I feel to just pour it all out and see what it looks like. I find that we are all so strangely interwoven with each other. It's both a crude and fascinating experience at once.

I use a lot of humor. At least I call it that. I mean some of it is just downright stupid, but mostly it serves an important function. For much of the socio-political reality we humans have collectively created is just so blatantly crazy. For instance, if you have any basic intelligence from a humanitarian perspective, you have to look at a guy like George Bush, or U.S. foreign policy for that matter, and just laugh at such gross absurdity.

But also, I feel that that being the case, the rawness of the general commentary needs to be cut with as much satirical content as possible. In the end I guess it's like they say - the hell with them if they can't take a joke! Because this book, like life in general, requires a flexible sense of humor.

In chapter one, I'm just sort of creating context and getting the ol' ball rolling. But by chapter two, I'm swinging away, like Barry Bonds surrounded by a skinhead mob. Chapter three begins the socio-historical and archetypal hunt for the pimp and the ho. I think you may view some of the findings as quite revealing. In chapter four, we will begin to consider how much room we will allow this whole thing, and how far it will go. Both archetypes have quite a role in the American dream.

By chapter five, it's back to some nitty gritty commentary. That's all you Americans respect anyway, no matter what you say. So we'll just break it down, even on a global level. Chapter six of course finishes this whole literary fiasco. I tried to offer some interesting philosophical overview, and even complete it all with a little "mind treat" for the developing gamer.

I have some background in the study of both Taoist and aboriginal philosophy. The relevance of Taoism is almost obvious here. Yin and yang make up the great cosmic dichotomy that shows up in all its myriad forms. To tell the truth, I don't believe I've ever read any Taoist literature dealing with the pimp and ho though. (Who knows? This might be a first).

Also in such a bizarre compilation as this, I have found that parts of aboriginal cosmology are always somehow relevant. Perhaps this work could even stimulate a little curiosity in the reader towards such an awesome and forgotten culture. And this would make an even more ironic impact.

I look forward to the adventure of all the discussion, which I have already started to encounter with this book. Some interesting points have already sprung forth in the dialogue I've shared with some associates who have worked on this project in various roles. Mostly I've seen the people who could deal with the conversation become more present to how real some of it actually is. They range from diverse economic and ethnic backgrounds, and identify in a multiplicity of ways, sharing layer upon layer of the socio-political factors involved.

I am certainly not interested in presenting myself as any kind of authority on anything other than my own experience. I have simply produced this book out of a sheer creative impulse. However, there are several works available that I recommend to anyone who wishes to do more investigation, or just explore more sources. I have included a list of relevant material in the back of the book.

Lastly, I want to be as emphatic as possible with the reader that I am not dealing with these archetypal roles in any gender specific sense. Anyone, regardless of their sex, can be the experiencer of these dynamics in various contexts. In Taoism, as well as many other philosophies, one learns that we are all comprised of both the masculine and the feminine dynamic/principle. Even the cosmos itself has both energies.

So I am requesting the use of your own intelligence to understand that I mostly refer to the feminine aspect with the pronoun "she," and the masculine with "he." However, you will often see I use a "he/she" reference, or "she/he," because I know that I have to continually remind many who will read this that *I am basically not dealing with gender specificity at all.* In this book, she is possibly a he and vice versa, in most any context referred to. Still, the dialogue is intense and confrontive like life itself, so I anticipate any and all interpretations and responses.

Whatever the case, I hope that mostly the reader will get some humor and a few insights out of the conversation. Or at minimum, it will just be a reminder that *the world in its rawness, given the opportunity, will be expressed!*

Peace be unto you..........baby!

Will the Real Pimps and Hos Please Stand Up!

Chapter I

"Is a $7 trillion defense contract enough? Can I come in now?"

"No!! Stay your ass out there and get me more money. And don't come in until I tell you you can come in, dammit!"

Who does the president *really* answer to? Does anyone know?

Chapter I

I Feel Like I'm Being Pimped!

"The costs of being a military superpower and waging wars around the world are high. Because hundreds of billions of dollars are funneled to the Pentagon every year, the government skimps on providing for basic needs of people here at home. Cutbacks in social programs have caused far more devastation in this country than any foreign army ever has."

Joel Andreas - "Addicted to War"

I'm sittin' here scribbling down a few notes on this project while the current speculations about our country going to war against the nation of Iraq are still reverberating through me. It was just this morning that I overheard the topic being discussed on the radio.

It's the predominant news story at the moment. And who knows? By the time you read this we may be at war or have finished them off. Yet it was only a couple of months before when there was the uncovering of the scandalous mega-corporate rip-offs taking place, perpetrated by none other than the C.E.O.'s themselves. They seemed to be plucking them like fat weeds in an open field - World.com, Adelphia, Enron, and a list growing longer by the day. Basically, it made many of us wonder if there's anything sacred at all in the financial fabric of what we call "the greatest nation in the world?" As it looks now, the answer is "no!"

And to boot, our beloved president was in fact heavily subsidized by Enron's number shuffling rascals during his presidential campaign. It's somewhat of a mixed blessing, but I'm at least astute enough to know that a war effort throws public attention off our internal scandals. And of course before Mr. Bush gets too closely implicated and his popularity points drop, he is again barking up the tree of Middle East conflict. You know, let's just pull ol' Sadam, the dusty villain, out of our Middle East closet of stretchable media topics.

After all, the American public hardly has a clue to what's going on all the way over in Iraq anyway. And mass psychology works such that people only learn to rely on what scraps of information they pick up on here and there. For the most part, we'll *act out* a greater knowing of remote issues than we actually ever have. And that's all we need - a bunch of bogus local authorities on the mid-east situation.

Yet this book is not to be so much about political manipulations and commentary, though such subject matter is only a total affirmation of the central concept. Rather it is a much broader look at "pimping" and "hoing." A look at where it may take place beyond just a street level context.

You see, I don't feel like I'm being pimped because I'm paranoid and suspicious, or because I've got some strange inkling about the matter. I can go to any fast food joint, or shopping center, or look at the real estate market for that matter, and just by experiencing the pricing system in our beloved capitalist economy, I experience a *direct knowing* that I'm being pimped!!

To most of my "peoples" from the "hood," the community of inner city experience that is, such a truth is none other than a given. It is "realer" than apple pie, or baseball, or the Star-Spangled Banner. "Oh say can you see...?" you sing. "Hell yeah, we can see!" is not only our answer, it is the authentic 'to the bone' experience. We can see who's playing the pimp in this political and economic game, and who is experiencing the other end of the pole.

But still this book is not about bashing the capitalist system in all its abundant glory and wretchedness, so please...check your counter-bashing responses for a moment. Just because I say capitalism out loud and tell the truth about it, it doesn't mean I'm against it or promoting it. It doesn't even mean I'm in such a conversation. It only means I'm being boldly honest about what *is*.

And that's what this reading experience will involve; raw honesty. ***For the pimp and the ho represent a very raw dichotomy of socio-political human relationship.*** You can talk around this dichotomy all you want, but you *cannot escape experiencing it* in some way in any large social environment.

So the focus here is not about making "pimping" or "hoing" wrong or right. To the contrary, it is about an honest exploration, examination and confrontation to bring us closer to being present to how these roles operate within our world and often ***through*** us.

So let's hammer it home further. "You damn right, I feel like I'm being pimped!" is my experience, because most hos know when they've been pimped, and have at least a general sense of *who* that pimp is.

You generally know at some level whether you consciously process it or not, if you're playing one or the other of the two roles in a given social/relationship context.

And just because I feel like I'm being pimped in one context, it doesn't mean that it is impossible for me to experience being the one "pimping" in another. So hey, at least there is *some* kinda light at the end of this freakin' tunnel (even if it is a dark red strobe).

A sense of levity will also be helpful in this exploration. For we will look a lot at what it means to state certain truths openly, and boldly, and how these truths may represent the boldness of a domain of life experience that some of us don't ordinarily live, while **others do and will by nature.** After all, someone's **got to pimp**, and someone's **got to ho.** That's just reality.

But it doesn't necessarily mean what we make it mean. Because I express that I'm being pimped, it doesn't necessarily mean that I see myself as being victimized. For 'victimitis' is an insidious self-collaborative syndrome indeed. And just because I may play the ho for a stint, it doesn't mean that I will find my way into the category of both a ho and a loser!

In the context that I experience being pimped, often it is more like the "playing field" of an evolutionary cosmic game. I am playing the role of the ho because **someone must play it** in the cosmic order of things. The more evolved into the game I may become, the more I may awaken to the reality that I can shift or "transform" the dynamics of my interaction with people and the world, such that I experience another role, like that of the pimp. And perhaps I can even experience it in a unique **new way**

- a way that's distinct from the more degenerate associations of its past.

For this whole evolutionary plot is quite elaborate. I mean even though President Bush, the "leader of the free world," is presently campaigning his way back into further mischief in the middle east, he ultimately has certain individuals he must answer to, quiet as it's always been kept.

And I'm not talking about the American public. Even the highest officials of the American government must answer to a small circle of multi-trillion and billionaire lenders. Now you can call me a wild "conspiracy theorist" all you want, but the national deficit is at so many trillion dollars now, and who the hell do you think that the U.S. government owes that to? Home Savings and Loan?

Look, this is not a book about the homework you haven't done on the history of imperialism, so you'll either be aware of some things that are said here or you can fill in your research as you get the opportunity.

I've told you this is a book about boldness, so there's not much room for punch-pulling. What you and I learned about as kids in history class was formally called *imperialism* and *colonial expansion.* People from the inner city call it *pimpin'* and *bangin'!*

The fact is President Bush and every other U.S. president has had their strings pulled by ultimate power brokers who only care to be known for their string pulling in certain *elite circles.* In relation to them, President Bush is pretty much just a "ho" himself...and he's the president! (So you could say Bill Clinton was then a "double ho" with all that he had going on). But let's not sidetrack too much.

Will the Real Pimps and Hos Please Stand Up!

If you can be the president of the United States and still be a ho of sorts, then we must be honest about the fact that all hos are not necessarily losers at all. After all, a ho usually does receive *some* form of compensation.

Let us take a look at another model. Let's say that you go to the most popular fast food restaurant in the world and buy a full meal. There's a pimp dressed up like a clown and his picture is displayed in full view, just so you know who's place you're spending your money in.

This symbolic figure and his co-rulers will offer you a quick "fix" basically- some minimally nutritious food that will certainly fill you up, if nothing else, at your own convenience. By the time the advertising and popularity has snagged your kids, they will feel like they have "been somewhere" after you have spent up your last few dollars buying them a few extra junk items. And of course all it will cost is about twelve hundred percent more than the clown-based ownership has paid for the belly full of filler and food coloring you've just consumed.

You're now happy, or at least full. And they're happy and very rich. The sign doesn't even read "Seven hundred trillion served" because it's not even necessary to display it anymore. No one doubts the pimping of ol' Ronnie. He's got a full staff of minimum age at minimum wage crankin' them burgers out almost round the clock.

Now you may only play the "ho" in the sense that you are the "have not" who must basically play the social game at the level you're at. The clown's food is what you could afford or "squeeze out" of the budget at the level you are at. Yet you have eaten. You have not necessarily been or experienced yourself as such a loser, or victim. You have simply continued to play in our collective mass matrix at the level you are at. You may be a "have not" in one sense, but you've *had* a burger in another. Being a ho doesn't mean being empty handed. It never has!

You see, most of us know that hos usually get something. Again, they pretty much have always been compensated on some level. It's just that the pimp has such an advantage over them in the domain of social power.

When you have a great advantage over people in social power, those who are less fortunate than you become fairly easy for you to turn into hos. *The political and economic state of the world screams this fact when viewed closely.*

There are very few governmental regimes in the world today that are not run by and ridden with political hos, sometimes referred to as "politicians." (Some would speculate that there might not be any). However, I would not even debate this issue because there are certainly enough politically powerful hos in the world to make my case a hundred times over. That's for sure! And any exceptions are very rare.

Leaders and officials are propped up to fill positions, which the most powerful *behind the scenes* pimps manipulate literally at will. The more openly "hoish" or representative of the people who pay them they are, the more agitative and demoralizing such officials are to the general public.

Take a man like George W. Bush, or "lil' ol' Georgie." He, like the rest of his party, obviously don't care very sincerely about the plight of lower income people, because he and his constituency are always on the exact opposite of the pole on each issue concerning poor people, and "minorities." He's not down with educational assistance or any form of mass upgrade in inner-city

Will the Real Pimps and Hos Please Stand Up!

communities (other than the police force). He doesn't ever consult poor people or minorities as a group on any foreign policy moves. And the only "reparation" African-Americans will get voluntarily out of he and his cronies is a couple'a bus tokens and maybe one or two retreads on the bus.

He is totally pimped by big business. It's not only disgusting, but to add to the layers of it all, a great many well to do Americans are wholly convinced that such stances on issues are very meritous. They actually believe it's all good, as if America has somehow pimped the world *innocently,* and the ***ultra-white view in the White House must be preserved in the world.***

They believe every word of propaganda that is slapped on paper or uttered by a newscaster, because *they just know* that their "moral majority" would not possibly connive and lie to them. Meanwhile, they're generally mislead further, *even when they quietly know* their leadership is lying to the public.

Look, the bottom line is it's all good anyway. Whether or not the president is lying, and the government is involved in the most perverted forms of corruption globally, it doesn't matter. As long as these "hoish" Americans get to keep their money and their wealth. They are pimped by propaganda and their love of wealth.

There is not much sensitivity to the global welfare, or to the human race as a whole. Though they may be rich, such a spiritual disposition is very much a form of (non-monetary) poverty.

You see, the pimp has an advantage over the ho in the domain of social power, but he (or she) does not have the advantage when it comes to core human realities like authenticity and humanity. Isn't there a famous biblical quote that reads something like, "What is it to gain the world, but lose your soul?" That sounds like both the pimp and the ho - you gain the world pimpin', but lose your soul hoing...hoing for the illusion you just gained. That's a cold thang.

The Christian church says the devil will buy you. They say Satan is always looking for and scooping up more hos. So I guess *it does not matter whether you're rich, or poor, or Christian. You can still be a ho in some way, shape or form!* And as a point of fact, while Jesus loved everybody, he *favored* the poorer downtrodden hos (He certainly didn't hang out with a bunch of rich folk).

For when you are a ho with political power and great monetary influence, you obviously get to pimp the poorer hos. So almost all of us can find a glimpse of ourselves somewhere in the scope of this conversation. It seems to go round and round like yin and yang, cycling through the multi-layered scheme of things. The pimp is thrusting and asserting like the masculine yang, and the ho is yielding, receiving and possibly fluid like the feminine yin.

The eastern philosophy of Tao (pronounced "dah-ow") states that it is best to have a balance of both yin and yang qualities for maximum longevity and wisdom in dealing with the life process. You need a little ho in you, and a little pimp to work with, and the sense and timing of when to step into either. A teaspoon full of ho and a tablespoon of pimp creates prosperity and balance. Now ask your spiritual guru about that, and see what kind of reaction you get!

While I sense I'm being pimped, I will not only laugh and be fluid, like a fluid/warrior/ho, but I will also become bold and self-defining like the creative pimp that I also am in certain moments of utter splendor. For *it is*

the pimp who creates his/her own reality, and it is this aspect of us, which creates the "world."

We Create Our Reality: From Metaphysics to Ghettophysics

Chapter II

Depending upon the point of view of the dreamer, the American dream will greatly vary.

Chapter II

We Create Our Reality: From Metaphysics To Ghettophysics!

"Life is a game in which the rules change as the game progresses, and you have to know where you are in the game to know what rules to play by. Furthermore, you can't ever be certain where you are in the game, and the rules don't always apply."
Brad Blanton - *"Radical Honesty"*

"Increasingly it has been found that our description of the world and how we think it works is confused with how it actually works. In other words, we so encapsulate ourselves within our world of ideas 'about the world' that we fail to 'see' the world as it actually is."
Malcolm Godwin - *"The Lucid Dreamer"*

This is not meant to be an excessively lofty conversation in metaphysics. It's to be kept as down to earth and straight forward as possible. We are creatures who interpret incessantly within the perceptual process we call waking consciousness.

Things take place in our field of awareness, and we interpret and assimilate the "what" of what takes place at a level so instantaneous and sublime, that we rarely if at all ever notice that we are doing such. I've just written a paragraph in this book, and I experience it that way because I've told myself that it is so, **and assemble it in my consciousness as such.**

If I were to tell myself instead that I've spent this last couple of minutes sailing in the clouds to the point where

We Create Our Reality: From Metaphysics to Ghettophysics

I believed and accepted it, then that would not only change, but also *create* my experience differently (whether I was in fact sailing anywhere or not). Do you get the point? What you experience is not just what is "out there" and "separate" from you, but also how your "doing" or interpretation/assimilation process creates the experience itself.

There is no extricating the act of interpretation/assimilation out of the process of our perception. There is no totally "objective" or "separate" universe out there.

The universe we say is "here" or "out there" or anywhere else is as much a product of our creative interpretation and fantasy/dream process as it is of some purely external stimuli. A physicist would refer to this as Heisenberg's "uncertainty principle," if you care to verify this truth. The principle states that you disturb or alter that phenomena which you attempt to measure with your assumptions about *how* to measure and the *cultural rules you impose* on the sensitive unknown domain of its origin.

Basically it means that process is both external as well as internal. That's the Tao baby! There is no external process without an internal one taking place as well. You see, I'm not just some dumb ho, so this kind of conversation can be handled.

Who defines for us where the universe begins and ends, or where possibility begins and ends? Who says the universe stops anywhere for anyone?

I'll tell you who, *the pimp defines and the ho operates within the pimp's domain of definition.* If the pimp says, "The world is flat," then the ho says, "Hey, I don't want to go over that edge." If the pimp says "We're going to categorize the global population as the 'first world,' 'second world' and 'third world,' then the ho says "Okay" And the territory labeled the "first world" naturally becomes the *top priority*. If the pimp says, "This is our definition of intelligence, and this is how we test and measure it," the ho says, "Okay, I will view myself and operate within that framework."

Take the African-American situation for example. We do not even say "whore" in urban America anymore. We say "ho." African-Americans are responsible for this. We created this shortening of the original English word "whore."

We have altered English and created our own original language form bit by bit since our experience of coming over here began. We had to. During the slave trade, African-Americans were forbidden to speak our own indigenous languages. If you were defiant to your slave master then the penalty would be death or torture.

English, not being our indigenous language, and not being taught to us formally, limited us. So over years and years we began to take European peoples' words and reshape, shift and encode them, as we were creatively and defiantly able.

This was and is an incredibly creative triumph in the midst of quite a struggle. For our indigenous grammatical and morphological language patterns were vastly different from those of European settlers. We not only struggle to use "proper" English because of our lack of access to quality education, we have struggled because English is literally not our "dreaming."

African-Americans don't create their experience in the same rhythm or flow or lingual texture as English or Euro-American people do. That shit is just real!

We Create Our Reality: From Metaphysics to Ghettophysics

And that's not an excuse. Many African-Americans can enunciate English almost better than the English, at this point. But again, a pimp defines reality, boldly and defiantly.

When the master said stay on the plantation, the would-be pimp had an impulse *to follow the impulse* to leave. As a matter of fact, he did! He therefore was a "bad" slave. When white society denied the African-American a right to equally participate in professional sports, you had the Jack Johnsons and the Muhammad Alis and the Jim Browns and the Wilt Chamberlains that have all come along.

When the American system says here's your political cage, a Nat Turner, Sojourner Truth, Frederick Douglas, Marcus Garvey, Angela Davis or Malcolm X comes along. When the American system says operate in a limited financial playing field and don't rock the boat, a Don King comes along. When we are continually oppressed and outmaneuvered in the judicial system, then the Adam Clayton Powell or Johnnie Cochran comes along.

When the American system says operate legally within these sets of laws, which are manipulated and modified at the whim of a wealthy ruling class, the inner-city street pimp says, "Yeah whitey, whatever you say."

The "bad" slave did not talk like the master (other than a diversion) because he or she was too busy creating their own reality. He was creating his own rhythm, flow and coloring of experience. He **reversed** words that **reversed his nature**, and **they then became applicable** to his nature.

"Good" therefore became "bad." Muhammad Ali is a bad dude. Nat Turner, Marcus Garvey, Frederick Douglas and Malcolm X were bad dudes. Sojourner Truth, Eleanor Holmes Norton, Angela Davis and Barbara Jordan are "bad" sistas. Johnnie Cochran is definitely a bad dude. And Don King is a straight up nut. He follows no one's rules but his own. He didn't even give a shit about his hair, and almost all African-Americans care about how their hair looks. Michael Jordan has defined the possibility of athletic endorsement for the globe. *It don't get no badder than that!*

Even Tiger Woods, who rightfully identifies with all of his mixed heritage, must have moments of utter defiance. For as "bad" a brother on the golf course as he is, you cannot tell me that he doesn't have a moment or two where he's walking down the fairway of the Master's (or some tournament) and saying to himself something like "Watch me whoop these white folks asses today!"

I know he doesn't think on that level ongoingly, because his focus has to be on playing a superb game. Secondly, I know that he's obviously not against any one group, being of mixed heritage himself. He's already privy to being exposed to more than one point of view.

But still, for all the experience he has dealt with in playing in the historically racist sport of professional golf, I know that there have been some moments that even a class act like Tiger is not interested in sharing with everyone. Tiger quietly and methodically shows white folks and everyone else who's the pimp on the golf course!

Now "Magic" Johnson and other entertainers and athletes are forging ahead as they acquire big chunks of the urban business market. These public figures continually redefine our view of African American possibility in the world, and in doing so also redefine it for the whole of humanity. So pimp on, pimp on my superbad brothas and sistahs!

We African-Americans really appreciate them being so "bad," because it's all good! They are so damn good at who they are and the reality they create. The world is not the same after them for all human beings. They are just that good. I mean bad!

And that is what I'm talking about. African-Americans have had to "pimp" the English language and make it work for us. *We must always strive to be "bad" in a "good" way, in a creative and defiant way.*

Defiance means bending the rules of the world quite a bit. For the world as we know it is only a set of rules. You can speak of certain realities in some cultures that don't even exist in others. So you could say that the "world" is created by not only the set of rules that you operate in, but the set of rules that operate "it."

For instance, you could say that all of the conversation in this book doesn't have a crap to do with the world. And from your experience, you may be telling the absolute truth.

However, by the same doggone token, I am an inner-city African-American male, and I have been all around the city, the state, the nation and overseas. And from not only my experience, but the experience of a great many who I've observed and learned from, the existence of pimping and hoing in the everyday world on so many levels is very real. That is why we talk about it in the way that we do!

The word "pimp" comes from the English language. It can be found in Webster's dictionary. If you want to know how formal or informal an English word it is, then go ask the king. People go to him to find out what the reality is of just about anything. They ask, "Is that the King's English?" *So he would be the logical one to associate with the word anyway.* Particularly from the point of view of "third world" people.

Inner-city African-Americans only use the word *in ways in which it applies to our experience.* The same with "ho." When we see some cat who has a lot of "game" going, legal or illegal, and is handling it powerfully or "puttin it down," *we may refer to that person as a pimp.*

It does not mean the individual has a stable of women that solicit money for sex. That is a pimp in the traditional sense. And we would all have to agree that that type of pimp is a real pimp indeed, and the original for sure.

But the term is used by inner-city or "ghetto" inhabitants to refer to a) the one who is a "have" rather than a "have not." b) the one who is sharp on following and manipulating the games of people c) the one who can be somehow attractive and has a flare to his "work." And d) of course the one who has others "get down" with him or her.

Recording artist Snoop Dogg breaks down to us how pimps maintain skillful emotional boundaries such that they can always remain keen and keep their personal advantage in the world. *"We don't love them hos" are famous words around the globe thanks to Mr. Snoop.* The words profoundly contain a whole philosophy evolved out of the inner-city struggle.

I emphasize struggle because obviously he's referring to some of the women of his own community. Some of the women who would, according to Snoop, certainly thwart his reign if he were to "love them."

Yet you love him all the while he's not loving them. How could you not love Snoop? He's authentic. I don't mean he does everything he talks about on his recordings. He doesn't have to. He pimps on another level now. He has become the icon of an important urban constituency- young, disadvantaged street kids.

Snoop is downright bold. He's bold, and he breaks the rules, and he's talented, and he charms you with his pimpish ghetto mystique. And all this is done with a ruthless, but somehow innocent flair.

The innocence is the realness. He's from the ghetto, so he can't be anything but ghetto. He's not attempting to "front" or mislead us on that one iota. Snoop is pimpin' straight, no chaser! He is a strange champion, because while he doesn't love "them hos," as he maintains, *he definitely gives us all back a lot of love just being who he is* – a brilliant creator of reality, rather than just a hardly noticeable repetition of the harshness and limitation of it.

I heard they were even talking about putting him together with some of the Sesame Street characters. You mean to tell me that this cat has came up out of his hood and pimped his way on to Sesame Street?

This is the kind of thing I'm talking about. *We use "pimp" to refer to a person creating reality. One who is "putting down the game," rather than having it put down for him or her.*

Now be aware that it still also applies to the broader degenerative context in which someone just basically exploits others. That where they would just misuse someone. Hey, that's always been pimpin' in a broader sense to all cultures.

But inner city African-Americans started the use of the word "pimp" in all of these contexts simultaneously. And

that is how we create the world – *by creating the world against its own rules!*
You have to. No matter who you are, much of what you have been taught will be inapplicable in the future, because *science or medicine or whoever will discover some new truth to tell you and you'll live thinking that that is so ultimately real, just like when they had early Europeans thinking that the world was flat!*
You have to just get down and create and pimp. You can't just wait for someone to say "Hey, I agree with you about how you're going about so and so." *Because a pimp is going to get down whether you agree with him or not.* Pimping is not about asking people do they agree. A pimp is just busy putting it down!
And so goes a conversation about pimps and hos. It's not about a polite debate. It's about America having pimped us and countless others for hundreds of years, *so now we're using her language like this!*
Let's take the word "nigger" for example. It's quite inflammatory in one context, and is used as a reference of camaraderie or endearment in another. If I walk into a group of white folks and hear the word "nigger" spoken in that historical tone that many African-Americans are familiar with, then I'm on alert. Something may be going down, or someone may have to vacate (namely me, depending on the numbers!)
But if I walk down the street in the "hood" and the "homies" say, "Yo, what's crackin' my nigga?" I feel supported and empowered by the love and brotherhood.
Which feeling is correct? The answer is they're both correct, and it was somewhat stupid to ask the question in the first place. Because it's not even about the feelings

being correct or not. It's obviously about the experience that there just *is* for people.

White folks created the word "nigger" and used it to define the African American's world or span of possibility. That none of them as a political body will formally take responsibility for it's origination and usage is not really of importance at this time. *That black people experience it as a reality almost all the time in some way, shape or form, is what's important!*

Since we have continually had to experience this reality, we have also continually had to get down and pimp, and recreate the word to be a different experience. The results are very strange.

If someone comes to America and doesn't know the ropes of racial relations, they will be quite mystified by the bluntness of the use of the term between African-Americans, while simultaneously noticing the hypersensitivity around the term being used in mixed group contexts.

African Americans generally like that this mystification exists. We like it that we feel comfortable calling each other "nigga" in one way, with a certain rhythm and flow, while others that we see as "outsider" groups do not feel comfortable at all using the term. *Niggas had to kick a lot of ass to create that dynamic!*

You see, this is a conversation about pimping. And the pimp puts down the game, and defines the rules, even when the game is called "the American dream." As a matter of fact, even more so when the game is the American dream. *Because the "American dream" is basically to pimp!*

Sure you can talk about a house, a job, a car, 2.5 kids and a doggy dog. But America was founded on pimping.

As a matter of fact, they could start the first chapter of American history in school on the subject of setting up a grand pimp's camp and doing some straight-up cross continental pimping!

Now that would be true American history. Instead of all this stuff about the pilgrims and how they eventually fought off the British, we could study how they just-a-kept them slave boats a comin', and just-a-kept that money a comin' in! *That's right, let's talk about what actually built this country, the richest nation on the planet.*

Sure white folks worked hard, but they generally had to get paid. They put down the game, (i.e., the rules, the law, the program, the "dream") that way. They were out pimpin' for real.

African Americans worked for hundreds of years for free or next to nothing!! You do the math. Whatever hundred million hours multiplied by a significant amount of money, versus umpteen hundred million hours at zero dollars per hour! White folks didn't build anywhere near the capital from their work that African Americans did during chattel slavery. If you can even fathom having hundreds of millions of people work for you for 200 years straight and you pay them nothing, absolutely nothing!! Then you can certainly glimpse what is meant by "putting down the game" or pimping at such a ruthless level.

Why they could call every chapter in the book series on American history, "Pimping!" Chapter one, "Pimping the Indians." Chapter two, "Pimping the Slaves." Chapter three, "Pimping the Colonists." Then "Pimping in the North," "Pimping in the South," followed by "Pimping on the Western Frontier."

Then supposedly Lincoln "freed" the slaves. So you could call that chapter "A New Form of Pimping." Then World War I came along, so call that "The Pimps Start Fighting Amongst Each Other Over Who Gets the Most Hos." Then the great depression, "Americas Hos Left to Starve?" World War II, "Stop Adolph's Crazy Ass, He's Trying to Pimp Everybody!" The Vietnam War, the 60's and the civil rights struggle, "Pimping, Partyin' and Co-intel-ho!" The Reagan years, "Pimpanomics!" You get the point. (My mechanic even said, "Don't forget about tricky Dick, wit his pimpin' ass!")

Because it's about who's creating whose reality, literally, moment by moment. In fact, you could say that if we are in the American dream, that is the collective psychic field of American people's visionary processes (both conscious and unconscious), then this "dreaming ground" or "field" is also very much, by its nature, a "pimping ground" or field.

You may think I'm over-using the term, but it's just to have us look *at* a few things, **rather than our usual choice of looking away.**

Think about how you are either working for someone who is capitalizing on your skills and talents, or perhaps it's the other way around and people are working for you. It may be both. You may have people working for you, and contract out to a bigger entity. Or you may be working for yourself. **In that case you have at least found a way to pimp your own skills and talents.** And if you think about it, even at times when you are very challenged, you need to *keep* your efforts out there on the streets until they pay off for you.

There is no "right" or "wrong" place to be. There is only the relationship and the dynamics that exist from moment to moment for you in the field of your profession, and in your social interaction.

It's not necessary to be personally against anybody or anything. Some folks just get tired of hoing and decide to "change the game." They can't really afford to waste time being mad because they got pimped. How are you going to be mad anyway at everyone who's pimping, and you're trying to pimp a little yourself at the same time? Now you know that doesn't make sense!

Plus you've got to realize, ***pimping is the hardest reality to break into after you have been so conditioned to just being a happy ho for so long.*** You're so used to just going along and having your reality shaped and set up for you by someone else. It doesn't take as much work to just humbly and mindlessly serve someone else's plan, program, operation or reality.

But you see, it's because the game of life is so vast and unyielding in its pace, and it is whatever it is for so many people from day to day, that you can't even worry about really shifting it as a whole. ***Pimping ain't gonna stop, you do realize at a very nitty gritty level.*** Even if you factor in the second coming, or Armageddon, or something of this nature, you know tomorrow, or the next day, or the next week for that matter, might not be time for the whole thing to go down.

So you know you've got to probably get your tail up, and get out (or stay in), and go to work. Cause as long as capitalist America is still rolling, somebody's getting pimped today and tomorrow, thank you! And now, just as yesterday and last year, and tomorrow, and next year, you get to choose. ***What role will I play in America? Whose dream is it?*** If it's supposedly mine too, then how is it showing up for me?

Because this is the real deal, right here, right now, moment by moment! And either the boat of awareness, full participation and fulfillment is passing you by, or you are on it, and not letting yourself be stopped by someone who ain't!

Raw Awakening

One of the crucial truths of creating your reality is that the world requires work to create. They say, "Nothing comes to sleepers but a dream." I say, "Nothing of real value comes to dreamers who only actively dream while asleep!"

For there are great truths that we are here to awaken into. Some of them have to do with learning to create a reality that doesn't already exist. In this you become the pioneer of a new reality. And this is a rare situation indeed. You must learn to become, as it is said on the street, "up on plenty game." *Street game and every other level of the game you can "come up on" (i.e. mental, political, economic, emotional and spiritual).*

This again is rare because not only are most people generally of a "herdish" type mind, but even those who leave the more frequently traveled paths of thought and originate still have to play along with the game, and often times, struggle in the system. They don't allow someone else to use up their time, talent and skill just because they want to. Rather *they ho because they have to, for at least a minute or so.*

The truth is, other than the pimps disregard and defiance of limitation, we would all probably still end up in the same loop. We would be waiting for someone to come along and put the program down. And yeah sure, that person or group might be somewhat benevolent and respected, but believe you me, they would ultimately put the program down on your ass! Because the world is just that creative a place if you work it as such.

For example, look how much violence and fabrication has been involved in the spread of religion. *As positive as so much of religious propagation is, there is always someone who is using it to pimp* (here it may be applied in both the degenerate and regenerate sense). And whether you want to deal with it or not, we all know that there are people out there who have been told to do everything from giving over all their money, to performing crazy sexual acts, to drinking suicide koolaid, to flying planes through a freakin' commercial building, all in the name of God! So though this may be a touchy issue to many, there's really no need to twist the truth any more than it's already been twisted. I'm just merely pointing to it.

For at the same time, there is certainly the vast and unquantifiable amount of goodness and salvation that has come from the work of religious people puttin' it down. It is almost unthinkable where we would be without it.

Yet everything about your reality changes from religion to religion. The whole plot of how you are even sitting here changes. Now think how many "religious people" are very benevolent and respectable, and yet they will put the program down on your ass if you are with it, or in many cases, even if you are not!

And I know some religious people may take offense to my saying this, but I will only remind them of how much time is spent by religious people themselves informing us about how some other religious group or doctrine *outside of their own,* is misleading and pimping others. So somehow it just seems like almost everybody wants to slide a little pimp in on ya.

Because people are about creating reality. Creating reality for you, me, themselves, whoever! And they will have you right up in their brand of dreaming. And some of it you may love, and it may truly be the greatest thing for you. While some of it may definitely not work for you in some ways, or at all. The sweeter they make it, the more comfortable you may become with it. Sound familiar yet?

No right or wrong is being dealt with in the conversation, just dynamics. But let us trace it back even further and see if we can get a glimpse at the ancient roots of these roles.

Chapter III

This is the Symbol of Tao

The yin/yang aspects represent unity through polarity. The two principles represent aspects of the same oneness, which reside in and emerge from one another. We are comprised of both principles.

Constriction	Expansion
Masculine	Feminine
Thrusting	Yielding
Rigidity	Fluidity
Light	Dark
Evident	Mystery
Particle	Wave
Solid	Flux
Pimp	Ho

Chapter III

From Whence Cometh This Pimping and Hoing Conversation?

"Whether we belong to a given group does not depend entirely upon our saying or agreeing to being a member of that group. We are part of a given "we" if the group's pattern is in or around us. Groups, like the fields around them, depend upon shared dreams. Everyone touched by a given field is a part of it."

Arnold Mindell - *"The Leader as a Martial Artist"*

I don't think that there is any specific anthropological or sociological date that we can look at and say, "ah yes indeedy, here is where pimping started to emerge." While many people have called prostitution "the oldest profession," I personally am still trying to figure out how in the hell that could be the case.

Why wouldn't we say that the trading of food, or tools, or goods is the oldest profession? What's up with some home improvement? What about getting your tent, your hut, your cave or at least a doggone mat together first?

I mean hey, I wasn't there, and obviously it's a tough call, but was it that one tribesman, or tribes "madam" possibly said to another tribesman, "Yo bra, you look like you could use one of them hook-ups. So why don't we make this happen before you get your little spot together and start gettin' your grub on?" I'm just not seeing it. But of course I could be blinded by the viewpoint of my urbanized lifestyle.

And yet it's not that I have to eat first before I get down all the time either. I know how to be spontaneous. But we're talking here about someone, however primitive, making an investment of sorts. And I know that's a crude, testosterone filled statement. But come on. We're talking about a situation maybe thirty thousand years ago. *I'm sure it was much cruder than we can imagine!*

Thirty thousand years ago there was no World.com, or Enron to even trip off possibly scamming you on an investment. Yet in this scenario we're talking about, *someone is obviously looking for a guaranteed momentary payoff!* So can't we at least rent a nice little cave, or chilled out little hut for a few hours? Sip on some nice coconut milk and relax?

Cause look, as morbid as this may be for some of you modern saints to listen to, I just want you to know, that I do not know, nor do I care to know of the sordid details. I'm not trying to estimate how all this might work as a documentary. Rather I feel it's crucial in our exploration to assemble some evolutional view of how these two precarious social characters came about.

One thing we can agree upon is that pimping is old. Very, very old! And I'm guessing that the first pimps would like for us to know who they were, and the pioneering work that they put down (knowing how pimps can be).

As well, we would have to speculate that the first hos would not want their limelight stolen either. Their work was just as historic and necessary as the pimps was in order for us to have this brilliant conversation and inquiry we are having now!

But alas, my research has yet to lead me to any even questionable documentation about either of them. The only exception might be a group of scientists who found a strange "cane" less than half a mile from one of the pyramids in Egypt. They say that the cane dates back at least fifteen to twenty thousand years. However, the scientists didn't even know enough *about* pimping themselves to determine how the cane could have actually been used. So we still don't know anything from this.

Let us see then if we can sketch what the make of these roles/types looked like early on. For while these two are very much *shadowed* by our culture, **they are also very much what the famous psychoanalyst, Carl Jung, would call "archetypal" in nature.**

Archetypal Origins

Archetypes are primary role patterns and potencies in the psyche. If you are not familiar with them, then you should know first off that you are actually very familiar with many of them. **For they express themselves through each and every one of us.**

They are what a "process-oriented" psychologist like Arnold Mindell might refer to as "rolespirits." See if these human archetypes ring a buzzer; the king, the queen, the warrior, the lover, the hero, the fool or trickster, the demon or villain, and on and on.

Mindell further explains that within the nature of group "psychic fields," we find certain kinds of polarized archetypes as well. Some are leaders and followers, haves and have nots, insiders and outsiders, supporters and disturbers, victims and oppressors, etc. *These roles emerge in all groups in one form or another.*

Any of these aspects of our "mythic" experience (that is our life story/adventure), can be played out in our personal or group process from moment to moment, depending on its course of unfoldment. According to the "Tao," process unfolds from not only what we know, but also from the utter unknown, from total mystery. So it may not be possible to predict exactly how groups will relate, or what role an individual may take from moment to moment within one. One who tends to govern or manage may be the group's "channel" for the king or queen to emerge. While one who struggles for a cause, or to grow in some sense may become the "warrior" momentarily. The artistic one, who is intensely connected with relationship and emotion, the feminine realm, is the lover. And the one who works with things on a somewhat mystical level, while often "playing" within process, may be the magician or trickster of the group.

Can you see how archetypes show up through us as mythic spirits needing to have a channel in order to emerge into the ongoing story of life?

If this is somehow making sense to you, *then perhaps you can see how the pimp and the ho have archetypal significance.*

Archetypal Origin of Pimp

Who is the pimp archetype? Who does he or she resemble? Well for one we can say that the pimp certainly resembles the leader, or the king/queen archetype, because he/she governs and is followed by his/her hos. A pimp cannot lack the capacity for leadership, or he will be turned into a ho as a matter of the natural process.

We can also say that the pimp has a great deal of warrior in him/her. He is definitely pimping for a cause. The only thing is, most of the time that cause is basically tied directly into pimping on an even ***greater*** level.

Now like the warrior, the pimp must struggle against many forces, both internal and external. The world does not yield more to the pimp than anyone else. For as any savvy gamester knows, "pimpin' ain't easy." But it is simply that the pimp has a special "knack"... a knack for pimping, that is.

The pimp is not only the leader of people, but also a leader with flare. Some great examples might be attorney Johnnie Cochran, Donald Trump or Sean "P. Diddy" Combs. While these men may not necessarily associate themselves with "pimping" publicly, in their own personal space they do exhibit an instinctual impulse to operate as such. And this is how they remain in the forefront of our view. It is the way they have masterfully put it down. Not publicly associating with being a pimp is part of their flare. They are the much classier type.

For while the pimp may struggle, he/she struggles to struggle less, not more. I don't think there is anyone who is not interested in this particular philosophy, but the pimp seems to have it down. ***Time is on the pimp's side, not against it.***

The ho, on the other hand, is usually worried. Because he/she does not "put down" the game, or truly call his/her own shots, the ho is usually having to experience life ***running behind.*** Sound familiar? I know I wish I could say that it doesn't.

But we only have so much time, true? There is only so much of the universe that we will have the opportunity to explore. So maximizing in quality and quantity is a perennial interest. So much so, one could speculate that if a gun went off a long long time ago to start off a race to see who could pimp the most, the world would look very much the way it does today. The pimp archetype would emerge on the scene as predominantly as the other universal archetypes.

The reason he is not as popular and acceptable to the mainstream as the others has to do with the nature of his power. For the pimp is shadowy, very shadowy. Because his power originated in the lower chakral area of the body and involves sexual energy, he has become very familiar with two human realities. One is the primal aspect and drive of the body. The other is the psycho-social taboo or boundary we call sexual sin.

The "shadow," in case you didn't know, represents the aspect of the self that is unacceptable intellectually, socially and aesthetically to consciousness. We all have a shadow. It's the part that doesn't fit neatly into the presentation of the "ordinary" self. And just because it doesn't seem to fit in the grand social plan, it gets closeted. Hence the term "shadow" applies, for the light of ordinary consciousness does not shine on this aspect of self.

Most people are not aware, at the level of surface consciousness, of their shadow. However, it will poke it self out from time to time. For instance, a person who is quiet and introverted all the time may have a rare drink or two, and suddenly become loud and uninhibited. Or a person who is sexually very conservative may enter a setting or mood in which their "freak," or primal sexual authenticity all comes out.

And it is in this murky world of the shadow that the pimp has evolved and attained an equilibrium which other benevolent or naive social types will never approach or confront, much less attain.

Perhaps we may not confront such a territory because of our traditional theological orientation. Whether one is of traditional Christian background or not, growing up in mainstream America we have almost all been fully exposed to a set of beliefs. Of these traditional beliefs is the heavily propagated Christian notion that we are "born in sin."

Now whether you agree with this or not, the fact is that the influence of such a concept on the human psyche is enormous. For we are born into a *body,* point blank. And if this body is equated with negation, sin and degenerativeness, then *who would* want to journey into its shadowy primal landscape? Such a doomful association would be enough to deter most.

But not the pimp and the ho, for sure. They both operate in a space of relative psychic freedom from such a concept, because in relation to conventional society and tradition, they are both defiers.

They *must* defy conventional society. They are shadow dwellers by nature. Therefore they view the shadow *in all of us.* They may view the charge that they are degenerative, sinful and wrong in who they are as the effort of another of their like, who's attempting to put the game down upon them. For one thing a pimp knows is that *other pimps come in all shapes, sizes and disguises.* And they usually see right through a professed theologian, or "authority" on god's will and message, when he or she, like them, is basically trying to merely play his or her own hand in the game. Religion is a reality, no doubt. But so are the many people who use it as a forum and hunting ground upon which to pimp.

Now besides being undeterred by the manipulative use of the concept of sin, the pimp knows that emotions have an even more powerful impact on a person's behavior than mere surface thoughts, or intellectual suppositions. The pimp knows of the powerful, shadowy impulses, inklings and urges of the body. And the pimp knows that no matter who it is, there is a possibility that these impulses could overpower that person's logical head-centered process at any given moment.

Therefore the pimp respects the one rule that can supercede all the other rules at any given point. This rule is basically that **wise and skillful pimping (usually) prevails.** And if it were not true, then the political and economic state of the world would be different than it is. But from the pimp's perspective, the hos of the world anxiously await!

Any and everyone can be charmed, and led by impulses into the pimp's world of bodily fantasy-based reality. The only lasting type of a resistance would come from a greater warrior-pimp, and possibly even a greater magician.

That's right. A pimp uses magic and believes in it. Now I'm not talking about the formal notion of hocus-pocus. I'm talking here about a subtle, but powerful charm. And I'm also referring to as much of a closeness as one can have to the deeper layers of life's mysteries. All knowledge, mystical, practical, technical, psychological and otherwise, will be employed for his/her cause.

From Whence Cometh This Pimping and
Hoing Conversation?

For all of this represents the expansion of pimping. And the pimp is down for this. So he will learn, with a sense of utter cunning, whatever he is capable of, including the esoteric.

King Richard had Merlin, the magician to consult with on his political and social affairs. Many world leaders, including some U.S. presidents, have had frequent visits with psychics and readers. The mega-power brokers of the world, who remain in clandestine circles and occult societies, use occult philosophy and even darker forms of witchcraft in order to maintain their power, wealth and secrecy.

Even the pop psychic, "Ms. Cleo" was eventually run off the air and out of business for pimping bogus skills on the "psychic hotline." And if you have lived in the Chicago area, then perhaps you are familiar with the legendary "Bishop Don Magic Juan." (Now here's a character who's hardly coming up short anywhere in the confidence department).

George Bush, like other presidents and rulers, *uses elaborate methods of creating illusion and misdirection, just like professional stage magicians.* This is because pimps know that a) reality often follows perception. If people view you as such and such, then they will respond towards you in the according manner. b) A ho doesn't have enough attention span to follow a skillful pimps ability to create illusion. And c) a ho's basic sense of curiosity is not powerful enough to solve the mystery that the pimp creates through his/her slickness and manipulative skill.

So we see in the pimp the king/queen/leader archetype, the warrior and the magician/trickster. He or she may have quite a broad dimensionality indeed. And to add to it, no one can deny that in the pimp, along with the other archetypical dimensions, is "the lover," as well.

The lover is close to his/her feeling or emotional nature. He/she dwells in connectedness and relationship. Feeling nature happens beneath the surface of external viewing, and is therefore likened to a sea with great depth, and of many levels.

The lover "feels" in a very deep and real way. The pimp feels in a very deep and real way. He/she feels very close to the game of life. He feels very close to his hos. He feels the call of life, the primal call. He feels the call to "have" in life, rather than life "having" him, and has to relate to the world as the creator of new rules and defier of old ones. *He feels the call to be with people.* You rarely meet an anti-social pimp, though there are a few.

For a pimp who rejects his connection with people becomes a very distorted figure internally. He distorts and degenerates because without his connection to people, he is less of an artist. This is why many are known to be very colorful. Their color expresses not only their power, but also their love of the art of life. Plainness, on the other hand, indicates an absence of power. A true pimp's world is never plain.

Further, a pimp's flare on the surface comes from deep within. He is already an abstractly seated character in the world, *so he must create powerful vibrations.* He must live an elaborate dreamscape. Vibrancy is key to his success and charm.

But the archetypal dimensions continue to unfold. And this may not apply for all pimps, for the world is full of a total array – from degenerate to regenerate, from very attractive to absolutely disgusting. But here again we are exploring the archetype in its broadest sense.

From Whence Cometh This Pimping and Hoing Conversation?

Every pimp creates his/her own reality. If he is able to do so in a constructive way, then everyone must at least acknowledge such a feat. They must acknowledge the pimp as a viable contributor to society, rather than the worthless unredeemable degenerate he has historically become associated with. In other words, the "constructive" pimp is as good a neighbor as any, and maybe even better!

In fact, not only throughout much of American history, but even in some smaller cities today, the pimp was and is regarded as a well-respected social figure. The mayor, city officials, police and prominent business people all hang out at the whorehouse.

But it is hardly anything that blatant in bigger cities today, and particularly when it comes to non-white peoples being involved. Pimping has somehow drawn plenty of stigma and adverse legislation toward itself over the years *since the money began to spread into hands that the government didn't want it to.*

Now I wonder how that happened? It looks like somebody had to change the game, because they couldn't keep a good pimp down. Well at this point, let's just say that the pimp has been *up and down* the social ladder. He has experienced both a higher and lower regard in the American social order.

Matter of factly, he/she is even a peculiar form of social hero. The peculiarity of the pimp's heroic nature comes from this paradoxical truth; he is also the villain. He is simultaneously the hero and the villain.

He is a hero in the sense of his social triumph. The pimp is a defiant winner. He has not only his cake, but his *cakes,* and eats them too! He is a hedonist with full access to the menus of the world. He is a "haver," not a "talker," or a complainer. He has somehow found a way to beat the proverbially ominous "system." The same grand system of society that gradually wears down all of its often barely distinguishable human parts, or hos that is. And to top it off, he does it all with flair. On the cover of a recent issue of Savoy magazine (October 2002), an African-American publication, a photo of the pioneer gangster rap star turned film mogul, Ice Cube, had the caption "Pimping Hollywood, and Loving Every Minute of It." The pimp is a hero because in a dreamland like America, no matter how mediocre or nightmarish it is for others, he continually pimps his way into an ever-greater dream. The greatest pimps even stretch the imagination, and set new standards.

Yet Ice Cube is the perfect example of the hero-villain paradox. *He only got to the level that he's at* by being the villain. After his emergence with the Compton based rap group, N.W.A. ("Niggas With Attitude,") his first solo album was entitled "Americas Most Wanted." It went instantly to the top of the pop charts. His genre is "gangster rap." His tag up until recently was "the nigga you love to hate."

A true to form pimp, Ice Cube's image and character was that of a rule breaker, an outlaw. And this is precisely heroic to our society. For we as human beings are all in fact dreamers, and our dreaming extends far beyond the domain of our conventional rules. *Pimps, even more so than hos, have no shortage of an inborn resource that we all need to be powerful in life- nerve!* Most of us learn to be quiet, conformative and underspoken early on in life. Most of our parents are hardly pimps, and even when they are assertive, it is within a conventional context. Subsequently this early patterning (as we know) carries itself out through the vast majority of our lives. Instead of "putting it down," we are more apt to "settle in" to a life routine. Once this takes place, the closest most people will come to the psycho-spiritual resource we call "nerve," will be a faint wish.

Not so for the shadowy unencumbered pimp. The pimp is a hero because he/she has the sheer nerve to play the social game and use any and all cards, without the burden of having to maintain a "decent" social image and reputation. He wears the villain identity with great flair.

So we now see quite a gamut of archetypes, including the king/queen, the leader, the warrior, the magician/trickster, the lover, the hero and the villain, are woven into the shadowy figure we call the pimp. The historical role of being a cold degenerate muscle man that alternately charms and then abuses women until their psyches become "brainwashed" and they solicit sexual acts, is well established. To this end the pimp has been a true villain. And yet from this historical character, there has evolved a broader more socially regenerate form of pimping.

It had to happen, because people are not experiencers of only one side of life. We all experience many sides, and live the energy and spirit of our environments. ***People are not just strictly from the category of goodness or badness, they are from the world of all-of-it-ness.*** And it is from this reality that there emerges many variations of such a figure, with the possibility of so many dimensions.

It is from this world that you get an Ice Cube, a Jay-Z, a Percy "Master P" Miller, a Sean Combs or even a Magic Johnson. This is how you get a whole class of bold and colorful wealthy people that are way too numerous for one book.

Far beyond the traditional "madam," and decades after the women's liberation movement saw a mass transition of women from homemaker to professionals of many sorts, *we see many of today's women pimping as "hard" as the men, if not harder!* This is the broader expression of this archetype, reborn in a new world, with new realms of possibility.

As for the misuse of people and resources by corrupt rulers and powerbrokers, "pimp" takes on the meaning of one who has gone even further than the small time "brainwasher" of women. In this degenerate context, a pimp is simply a grand, conniving, exploiting, manipulator of people. And this type of pimp has been around in all cultures, and is recognizable throughout history.

Here you will not find much archetypal dimensionality. For instance, I don't see much flair or the lover in a George Bush. But then again, I'm only looking through my own eyes. Who knows what older conservative white women see in him? Hell, they voted for him! He may actually stimulate them. With what, I don't know. But I guess somehow...?

Bill Clinton on the other hand, has all the archetypal dimensions. He's much more of the new, broader expression of a pimp than his conniving, colorless, ruthlessly conservative successor. He's almost in the category with cats like Cube and Snoop Dog.

From Whence Cometh This Pimping and Hoing Conversation?

Archetypal Origin of Ho

Now we know that the ho goes way way back. But let's look at her archetypal roots, shall we? After all, most of us are just everyday hos in this American system. So let's take an interesting look into ourselves, in a way that we probably haven't up until now.

Who is the ho? She definitely ain't the queen. The queen is a pimp baby, that's for sure. Look at the queen all the way over there in England. Parliament and everybody else bows down to her. She is the core of an aristocracy which is a thousand years old or more. Those people would probably lock you up if you called her a ho.

Hell, England used to look at America as one of her hos that just absolutely got out of hand. We don't even speak the King's English anymore, and damn near don't care. *America herself is evidence that your biggest ho can eventually become the biggest pimp.* But let's not sidetrack. Suffice to say the ho ain't the queen, and is yet to be anywhere in the near future. (Now if that changes, you write a book and let me know).

The ho is not the leader either. Maybe she can lead some other hos parading around a small radius, but other than that, she is no leader. And a dumb ho will get you into some really silly stuff. So just beware, that's all I can tell you.

However the ho has a great deal of warrior in her/him. Remember the warrior struggles to prevail against forces. The warrior struggles for a cause or to grow personally.

Now the ho is a fundamentally whole and complete person, a divine being and all that. Except she/he ran into the pimp one day and her trialsome path had to emerge.

If the pimp operates in the thrusting, firm, issuing, masculine energy of yang, then the ho operates in the yielding, fluid, receiving feminine energy of yin.

At her/his best, the ho is fluid. Those of you who identify with being pimped by the system know that from day to day, in the harsh grind, fluidity is key. You've got to "roll with the punches," and keep it moving. Talking all that abrupt nonsense about "I'm through with this, I ain't dealing with this shit no more!" might be what you feel inside from time to time, but you'd better temper all that with some fluidity and carry that ass on to work at the factory, or push that paperwork until you can create something more viable.

Because a ho has got to struggle for real! So she/he has to develop the inner strength, and fluidity of a warrior. Hell, I'm writing this book while sitting in my truck on the side of the road. I've got to carry my happy ass into work right now. That's how real this is.

A ho is a warrior who must carry the burden of humanity's inhumanity. As a ho, you have to deal with the fact that there are way too many pimps out there, and they are ***all trying to find a way in which to pimp you.*** Even other hos are trying to get their pimp on, so that they can get out of hoing themselves.

People who don't even have any business trying to pimp at all, are out there just tripping. I'm telling you the shit is crazy. And here you are just trying to do your little thing and somehow be content.

Any experienced, down to earth ho can tell you for sure that human beings as a group are crazy. Human beings will pimp anything that moves. Then, we will pimp anything that we *can* move. There just is no statue of limitations when it comes to human beings' inhumanity

From Whence Cometh This Pimping and Hoing Conversation?

to other human beings. So a ho knows in her heart that she must bear the brunt of this reality. Because a pimp ain't bearing the brunt, he's issuing it!

Still, you got to give it up to the ho (give her much credit), for she/he stays in the game. And this is what is most important. Because we all know that once you're out of the game, you're either dead, or so far back you might well consider just trading your shit in.

The ho, in fact, has to be admired for her gamefulness, her fluidity and her attitude. She is positive even in a world that is very negative. She/he fulfills her daily tasks, no matter what, like a good ho. She is often more loyal than Lassie, even when it is sometimes to her detriment. This great nation we inhabit today, was in fact built by the magnificent work of her hos. The pimp, of course, created the idea. But the ho did all the footwork.

And that's why you've got to have them. You can't have a good party or build a strong nation without some hos. Maybe that's just the pimp in me expressing that, but we've got to keep it real. Hos are like sugar frosted flakes, they're grrrrrreaaattttt!!

And you know it's true yourself. Hos will get your party jumping. If you just invite a bunch of pimps, then they will spend the whole time absorbing up all the energy, and drawing all the attention to themselves. Listen to me though. You don't want just a party full of "P. Diddy's" or "Cubes" or "Oprahs" or whomever. Hos bring life to the situation.

See, I know how it is. Everyone wants to sit around and bad mouth all the hos. They want to say she's not this and he's not that. And well maybe so. It's probably true. Okay, it is true. But what's more important is not that she's **not...**, it's that she *is*, period. Hos just are.

Will the Real Pimps and Hos Please Stand Up!

Take a course in modern existentialism if you don't understand the philosophical significance of what I'm saying.

Hos exist because we created them. We literally "dreamed them up," as Mindell would put it. They are a part of our collective psychic make-up, just like kings and queens and warriors and lovers. As a matter of fact, *the ho is the lover, extraordinaire.* And talk about having an archetypal thread woven through you.

The ho is full of humanity. Moreso than the pimp, because the ho is full of love to be given to whomever. While everybody's walking and talking like their boo boo don't have no stench, the ho is just being real. She/he deals with the stink of the posturing, self-status raised, "honorable" community folk in as fluid a way as she deals with the struggle of it all. She simply chalks it up to a game in which the key point is to just remain in it.

The ho is, like her counterpart, a very shadowy figure. She loves the body in ways that our conventions restrict us from talking about. She loves the shadow, and nutures it. This is why many people who are in relationships often end up at a point where they only feel able to let loose and express their whole self when they are with their ho.

You see, you can act like you are so put off by this type of a conversation. *But not admitting that your shadow is there only makes it larger, and more neglected or repressed.* Eventually, if you repress it enough, then it will become very distorted.

Look at how all of these Catholic priests have proved themselves to be worse than anything you could associate with a pimp or a ho. They could not deal with their own God given sexual nature in a healthy open way. So they

From Whence Cometh This Pimping and Hoing Conversation?

repressed the energy that would eventually find a way to leak out and express itself. Only by then, their shadows had been repressed for so long, they became very distorted and grotesque.

If only they would have been more honest. Rather than trying to project themselves as being so holy and closer to God, they would have discovered that God gives us *all* a shadow, and therefore we all may have a little ho in us somewhere.

Instead of getting their groove on in a non-destructive way, they went after little kids. All the while looking down on who they could have counted on for sure. Why you silly pastors, that's what hos are for!

Unfortunately, the more macho and testosterone intoxicated we get, the more we disconnect with the mysterious sea of our own body and feelings. The truth is, the ruling patriarchs have never wanted to acknowledge the "goddess," which represents the divine feminine principle of the universe. *So a poor ho could hardly stand a chance of having any significance.*

Still, who will be the humble healer of our global shadow? While the testosterone frenzy of war-mongers like Bush and Sadam and Osama and whoever else who has a weaker game at authentic humanitarian love than they do at missile launching, continues to dominate, we are only increasing the same karmic dynamic which looped us into the nonsense in the first place. Indeed, while pimps are brilliant, they can also become easily imbalanced by their own power. And just as only yin balances yang, there's no one who can balance a destructively spiraling pimp, but a positive, intelligent and resolute ho.

Will the Real Pimps and Hos Please Stand Up!

Oh yes, they do exist. And in fact, in this case we must appeal to the American public. The sleeping ho must awaken. And if shock is what it takes, then so be it. *For we must be more responsible hos.* Because guess what? The pimps in Washington ain't going to change, and you know that's the truth.

They have to be called out about all of their Enron's, and every other piece of filth they're involved in, foreign and domestic. Well, maybe a little filth can stay, but you get the point. (Nothing wrong with a little filth, I always hold).

But these cats in Washington are just bitch-slapping us. And meanwhile, we're so busy "frontin'" to the rest of the globe, as if everything's all good over here in America, just because we get treated better than the rest of the world's hos. Come on bitches, I mean people!

Anyway, I almost got sidetracked. (But not so, for we are speaking about none other than *the mythically infamous ho).* And speaking of the ho, she is certainly a magician of sorts herself. At the street level, she is known for "turning tricks." Now you may not necessarily want to see the kind of rabbits she's pulling out of her hat, but she's got to pull them none-the-less. So if you are in the company of a ho, you must pay close attention, or before you turn around, she may turn you into her next trick.

For hos work in the shadow realm, just like the pimp. Processes are not "ordinary" in such a realm. They are "otherworldly." For instance, a person may find themselves in the company of a prostitute and not even know why. Though lower chakral energy is involved, sex may not be the only agenda.

From Whence Cometh This Pimping and Hoing Conversation?

People are drawn to the primal mystique of the unknown. The often dry machinery of ordinary life hardly adds up to an experience of the totality of being. So many are drawn by deeper impulses to explore their shadow zones. These "zones" would be places and innerspaces that are somehow perceived as forbidden due to the implanted doctrines of acting moral authorities within one's tradition, or simply to general social taboo.

The world of the "on-the-go-ho" is swift, shifty and alluring, just like the flashy handwork of a stage magician. Yet people are not drawn to it for prestige. That would obviously be the pimp's domain. Rather, they are sublimely overtaken by the spontaneous, sensuous, open, melodic flow of the hos world.

You may even recall a time when you were on your way somewhere, but not pressured by a time schedule, or maybe you were just plain hangin' loose, and somehow you just found yourself kickin' it with some hos.

Somehow you just relaxed into it. There was no boss around, or work schedule. There was no one to pretend you were all this and that in front of. And even if there was, you weren't in the mood. And you knew you were in the company of some hos. But you weren't trying to hide anything. *Because hey, everyone knows deep down the world is a ghetto anyway. And the ghetto ain't nothing but everyone's shadow; the truth we create, but keep managing to inappropriate.*

So you were just having a drink and running your mouth, and hangin' out just basically being a ho yourself. Had somebody jumped out and caught your ass on camera, you couldn't say shit but "Hey, you damn right I'm having a good time, now get that camera outta my face!"

Because a ho knows how to have a good time. She doesn't have to carry the weight of pretense (though some dumb ones do). She follows her impulses and her body into many adventures. And while we all deplore street prostitution and its destructive reality, we do generally accept hoing at a higher more socially integrated level.

Many hos have regular jobs and just "work it" in all their relationships. They may have several incomes, and you don't know exactly how they do it. There are many a smooth ho out there who've got it going on. And how could you blame them. The pimp has many things, and runs the game, so naturally a ho wants her/his share. She's a "have-not," relative to the pimp. But when it comes to having nothing, a modern ho truly ain't having that! She's got to be free to be!

She is still about freedom, even though the pimp puts down the game. So you could say that the ho puts down "the game within the game." And as the often barely differentiated parts of the American system, we all can relate to having to put down a game within a game.

Attention All Hos: Beware of Patriarch!

Yes, that's right. Even with all of your red, white and blue on, you will utilize every tax loophole you're tipped off to, because you know the rich pimp, I mean American citizen, is doing it too. So you don't want to be counted out, you want to be counted in.

You want to be counted in on a little of everything that that little hypocritical pimpin' ass patriarch told you was so forbidden. Because if he told you it was "forbidden," then there's probably something to it that he's getting out of it! And all the while, he's squeezing everybody else for every inch of service, allegiance and money he can get out of them, so that he can keep all the P.E.A.S., as my streetwise uncle says. (That's *P*leasure, *E*njoyment, *A*nd *S*atisfaction!)

After all, you know the patriarchy may generally do some benevolent pimping too. And that's why you can't stand against it on a lot of things. But as a ho, you already live outside the rules, *so you are more able to peep the whole game from your vantage point.* And you know that the patriarchy's game is to pimp, point blank.

It's the natural order of things. Because the one game that has *already been put down in the universe,* is the same game *that's ongoingly being put down in it.* And in this game, which is as profoundly momentary as it is eternal, the pimp and the ho do their dance.

The feminine principle must operate with the dance that is put down by the masculine one. Sometimes it seems unfortunate that this is so, but just as there is no yin with no yang, there is never a ho without a pimp, and vice versa.

Somebody's got to put down the game, and *someone has to represent that which receives, flows with it all, and keeps it real.* The truth is, if it weren't for the feminine principle, the feeling depth of our beingness, there would be nothing but a bunch of inauthentic, crazy, lying ass pimps out here running amuck.

But fortunately we are moving into the Aquarian age, and this means things will be moving into a greater balance. We are experiencing a shift into a greater awareness of the divine mystery that the universe is, and of the great necessity of understanding the feminine principle.

It's not just about the dogma of the patriarchal pimps of the world being "right" about everything that they have told us. Sure, they are still puttin the game down, but more and more, the hos are getting back into it. With every natural and holistic truth that is brought to the forefront of human consciousness, we find an expansion of our belief and viewing system.

For over a thousand years, we have been pimped by the growing materialistic paradigm and accompanying moral code of hypocrites. They talk about the one who is without sin "casting the first stone." Hell, you gotta be kidding me. There is so much sinning in so many forms, and so many stones out here flying every which-a-way, nobody knows about being without sin and who cast the first damn stone!

Look, if you are a ho, and you get picked up on the social grid (which you will if you're out there hoing), you're getting your ass stoned, point blank. This is the indirectly written, hypocritical, pimpin' ass patriarch's moral code – stone all hos!

And by "stoning," it doesn't mean people actually throwing rocks at you, like in the old days. "Stoning" refers symbolically to *indicting*. Stoning all the hos, as the patriarchal pimps have put it down, means morally, spiritually and socially indicting them. *It means clobbering them with a guilt factor.*

It's a brilliantly manipulative game. Because as long as these degenerative patriarchal pimps make sure that there is an uninterrupted moral and social conversation about the guilt and wrongfulness of hoing, people's attention is diverted from their pimping. It's the perfect misdirection play- a form of psycho-political slight of hand.

From Whence Cometh This Pimping and Hoing Conversation?

While we're all busy throwing stones at hos (indicting them that is), we have failed to realize that the "hos" we are throwing stones at will be interchangeable with ourselves in one sense or another, at one time or another. And when I say "we" in this context, I'm obviously not making a general reference to a huge group of pimps. Because pimps don't usually run in herds, hos do. Pimps are the ones doing the herding, right?

And now they've herded us into a perennial conversation about the wrongfulness of ourselves in some sense or another. Pimps do this to hos all the time. That is, they herd us into a conversation, when *the point isn't even in the very conversation they've herded us into.*

What in the hell is wrong with hoing? Absolutely nothing! Now who you ho *for* may be an issue. And of course *the way* in which you presently ho may be something you want to reconsider. But if anyone tells you that there's something fundamentally wrong with hoing, they've probably gotten it directly or indirectly from some pimp. I mean look, if you're out there hoing, then that's just the existential predicament you're in – you're a ho, straight up! But that doesn't mean you need everyone to just all out come down on you. Hos don't need chastisement. *They need coaching!*

And you see pimps know all this in the first place. But the pimp, being the skillful overviewer and herder that he or she is, also knows that hos don't know all the answers to how the game is put down. That's how they've ended up hoing.

Instead of "would he who is without sin, throw the first stone," there might read elsewhere "would he who is without pimp, sit back and watch all the hos (manipulated into) throwing stones at each other." For the pimps' magicianship by definition exceeds that of the ho.

And again, there is generally nothing wrong with hoing. Hoing just is. But it is the patriarchal pimp who has everybody viewing the universe in the narrow and rigid context of right/wrong polarity. Truthfully the greater amount of process in the universe occurs beyond the rigid context of right and wrong, black and white.

People are basically just "being" and exploring the vast mystery and reality that is available in this bizarre *living,* multi-universal system where we are all intricately, paradoxically and yet profoundly woven into one another. Hoing is just another path one finds oneself on in this incomparable odyssey, this bizarre adventure.

It is hardly a matter of wrongness or guilt. You are born into an environment that acts as somewhat of a "cosmic information cocoon." ***The information that you are exposed to shapes you, and you make choices in the midst of a life journey that is more than anything else, an exploration.*** Depending on your matrix of probability, which involves heredity, environment, education, social interaction, financial and other resource access, and of course pure chance, you may end up anywhere from one who experiences being a ho in the remotest sense and the remotest instances, to an all out full-time skank.

In any case, operating from a conversational starting point of guilt is usually the utter result of an implanted psycho-social model in which you are inherently entangled with such a position. In other words, far beyond our authentic transgressions, we learn to spend so many of our precious, living, breathing, and waking moments feeling guilty.

The fact that either you yourself, or someone, or many people that you know experience this truth is the only necessary evidence. The game is no less than real. You see, only hos of a certain financial status can afford to see a shrink, if they feel the need. The rest of us must simply keep on pushing, no matter how adversely we are viewed by the world or ourselves at any giving moment.

Thus a ho must have a heroic resolve, even if he or she is the only one who will view his or herself in such a way. The world has traditionally viewed her as the lowest rung on the social ladder. And for thousands of years, she has been symbolically crucified upon that rung by the pimpin' patriarch.

One of the ultimate heroic models is that of the Christian's Jesus. He is reported to have been a victim of a crucifixion. Its portrayal in many art forms from paintings to literature to film is renown. And one of the most distinct impressions one gets from viewing these depictions is that being crucified is an incredibly lonely experience. It is also reported that he "died for all the sins of mankind," and this would include those of pimps and hos alike.

Many a ho has an experience of loneliness in the world, despite her/his many associations. Her form of heroism is similar in that there is great devotion involved. Part of that devotion is simply a devotion to identifying with hoing. That is, identifying with being a gameful underdog in the pimps world. The other part is the devotion to the *service* that goes along with hoing. **Hos are born to serve.** Serve their country, their employer, their leader, their given set of ideas and beliefs. Hos are born to serve any and all forms of pimps. And in serving their pimps, they serve the world. For who else puts it all down in the first place?

Ho My Goodness, Hero and Villainess?

By themselves, with a small platoon of other hos, or in great mass, they keep the world turning. And in this sense, the ho is truly a hero. But she/he, like the pimp, is a shadowy paradox. For she too is a hero and villain simultaneously. If she wants to, she can act in such a way that even the average villain would be given a cool headache. And let me tell you, you really don't want to mess around with a truly troublesome ho, for real!

I mean let's be honest. A lot of these hos out here ain't worth a damn. They're out here just giving hoing a bad reputation. And really, we know that hoing already has a bad reputation. So they must be out here doing too too much! Hell, the number of stones being thrown goes way up when some of these hos step out on the grid.

And a lot of these crazy hos have the nerve to take pride in it. True enough, hos can be fluid. It's part of their "yin" nature. But now they will take the notion of fluidity to the maximum. Many a ho can easily play the villain with fluidity.

Unfortunately, even the nicer, more positive hos must accept their "stoned" fate as well. For many of them however, the role of the villain has a more playful and intriguing slant. They may be the delight filled "tasters" of the forbidden fruits of life. You might see one of their well-compensated set of lips on the video screen or a magazine advertisement. They're paid out and laid out with plenty of goods. They are the pinnacles of their path, for they are the glamorous ho.

Glamorous hos are certainly imbued with great magic. They enchant and enspell us. Take Marilyn Monroe for instance. I mean I know she was an accomplished actress and all, but come on. She took it all the way to the very top. And put it right on the president's desk! J.F.K. sure didn't wait for congress before he put his signature on that. And Robert stood behind his brother, and then gave his *full commitment* to the matter. Because no matter how much turmoil there was going on in the world, she went straight to the top of their political agenda. Hell, Marvin Gaye hadn't even wrote, "Sexual Healing" yet, and they were singing it.

But Marilyn still enspells, turns heads and has a following to this day. If they had a hos hall of fame, you know it would be filled up, but she would've had to receive the top honor of merit. And the hall itself would probably need to be the size of the damn pentagon, and expandable. So I'm not trying to deal with that list.

I'm only trying to make a point. The most talented and glamorous hos are not penalized. They are revered and rewarded. Look at how many of Hollywood's great names started out in pornographic films, including Joan Collins, Chuck Connors and Sylvester Stallone. You can't be mad at them because their path was what it was. Besides, they're either pimping the game now, or they died pimpin' it.

You've got to consider that hoing in one form or another might not be the worse move you can make. Look at Vanessa Williams. She was America's sweetheart. The first black woman to win the coveted Miss America title. And then she was stripped, because the white folks who were running the pageant said "whoa Vanessa, whachu been out there doing?" Somehow one of America's biggest outright pimps, Bob Guccionne, owner of *Penthouse Magazine,* had gotten a hold of some photos showing Vanessa being naughty by nature – shadow nature that is! And his ruthless ass wasn't about to hold up the press on this one.

Well they tried to make it look like it was over for Vanessa. But the cosmic order had it different. Instead of being penalized for hoing, and then having it all go down hill, Vanessa's popularity was not only sustained, *it increased.* And the girl has so much unstoppable class, talent and dimensionality to boot, she came out smelling like "essence of rose of olay!" And in that sense we must acknowledge that Vanessa is now one of the classiest of the class of pimps.

Mr. Bill Clinton, on the other hand, is another story. He's my man. And a lot of black people felt that way, because Bill was just cool. You could identify with his coolness. He smoked weed, played sax and was very youthful in his appearance (compared to most of those decrepit looking presidential cronies). But the thing about Bill was that as much of a pimp as he is, and as much as he liked to hang out with hos, Bill just got to hoing a little too much himself. At least that's how the big pimps in Washington saw it.

For ol' Bill took the concept of "multi-tasking" to a new level. He gave the phrase "leader of the free world" new meaning. He'd be talking on the phone and have an ambassador to some country on one end, all the while fully kicked back in his oval office chair, with young Monica on the other!

I mean even black people couldn't argue for his case, because Bill was just too far out there. In the end, even though my people were much more optimistic when he was in office, we couldn't stop his ass from being utterly stoned by the whole damn country. I mean really, no matter how I see it as a black man, America feels this way – if you're going to be the president, ***then you've got to create the basic perception for the world that you're the biggest pimp, not the biggest ho!***

But Bill, all I can say is "brush them stones and pebbles off your suit, and out of your hair brotha, cause many of us still got respect for you homey."

Now for the average ho out there, being a villain is less of an issue than paying bills. You just go through life working your ass off, quietly alternating between being somewhat of a hero one minute, and feeling a bit "villainy" the next.

Your average everyday working class ho is just cruising it on in. She or he may not have gotten to play the big pimp this time around, or even the most glamorous of her like, but one thing's for sure – like a true underspoken hero, she/he will keep pushing and chalk it up to experience. You ho and learn.

And there we now have somewhat of an archetypal portrait of the ho. We know she's the warrior, lover, magician, hero and villainess. And we know the great span of her/his global playing field. We have also glimpsed the archetypal playing field of her counterpart, the pimpster. Some of us may even become more aware of these paths in our own personal mythic plot. But now we will see if we can glimpse where this whole bizarre odyssey may lead. For in spite of all else, we must continue to evolve.

Will the Real Pimps and Hos Please Stand Up!

Introducing the
2003
Ghetto-Famous
Pimp Gallery

Just a few of the "who's who" in puttin' it down.
Compiled by E. Raymond Brown.

Don King

Now this brother here embodies practically every dimensional characteristic and nuance that one could possibly embody of a pimp. He's a genius, a nut, a strategist, a rule breaker, an innovator, a leader, a communicator, a slickster, a powermonger and a downright filthy rich ass fool! He's America's unconsciously dreamed up alter-ghetto freakin' pimp ego. Why he's, he's.........he's Don. A pillar of character in the pimp's gallery. Donnie baby, what can I say? I guess we have to love yo crazy ass......."Only in America."

George Bush a.k.a. Lil' Georgie

    Here we have the biggest degenerate pimp that we can lay our agitated little ho-sights upon. So George, look, I know that guy wrote that book insinuating that you're a stupid white man. And really, what's behind all that is…basically, it's the truth. I mean we know you obviously have some intelligence, somewhere. If not, your Daddy's got it, because he ran the C.I.A. at one time, right? So he'll just tell you what to do, like he always does anyway. Because if you really wanted to bag the biggest terrorists, you would just go on and lock him and yourself up. But hey, don't get your little ears steamy over ol' E. Ray baby. I'ma give you some room to grow…..grow a foot up yo ass! Cause I'm tired of walkin' around with yours up mine, and everybody else's I know.

The 2003 Ghetto-Famous Pimp Gallery

Bill Clinton

Well, well, well, "still Bill." Still pimpin' Bill Clinton! See Bill, they just wasn't ready for where you were really takin' 'em. But I could see your vision baby. You had *VIS-E-OWN!* It might have been a little blurred for a minute there, gettin' down wit all that Monica drama like you did. But you can sho see clearly now, brothaman. The rain is gone! And I don't know what kind of "knowing" you work off sometime. But I bet you anything it incorporates both a little metaphysical and plenty ghettophysical! Man, Bill, you can hang out with the brothers all you want. Because you passed all the requirements of the "Ghetto Pimp Ass Presidential Initiation Phase Test." And honestly, there wasn't one until you came along. You caused us to even go forward and create it, witcho ghetto-political ass.

Oprah Winfrey

Excuse me, but I've only got one question for you Oprah. How in the hell do you get to be the richest woman in the world? Number one, number two, does it really matter? And don't sit up there looking all sweet, primped and dignified and tell me you didn't have ta do some serious heavy-weight, behind-the-scenes pimpin'. White folks in America ain't hardly trying ta let no black woman be the richest woman in the world. Why if I could scoop some of the dirt you walk on, I'd hang on to it, cause that must be some hellava dirt. 'Cause you got it all mama, including 'ol steady Sted. And all you've got to do is just keep telling him he's as much of a pimp as you are, and he'll be okay. It's just a little man thing.

And furthermore, I know you'd probably never say it publicly, but honey I understand how you must feel about all these triflin' jaded ho-ass critics of yours out here. But you've got way too much class for them, so let me say it for you – "Why, they can kiss your big royally empowered black ass!" Nuf said baby, pimp on witcho bad self.

The 2003 Ghetto-Famous Pimp Gallery

Donald Trump

This savvy little slick-ass white dude hasn't been in the town talk the way he used to be in the 90's, and he doesn't need to be. He did so much pimpin' in that decade alone, he's got my respect and whole bunch of other people's, you know what I'm sayin'? Don was pimpin' the whole game so beautifully, even when he and his wife broke up, she was doing her thang, pimpin' off all the popularity. That's tight when you got it so tough you can transfer the pimpin' like that to people around you. I ain't mad at you Don. Quiet as you've been living, I know that means you've only been putting it down tougher and on a more vast level. If you decide to make a tape series on "How to Pimp in American Business," it's essential that I get my copy and add it to the collection playa.

Johnnie Cochran, Esq.

Damn Johnnie! You could just put "Mr. Johnnie-Pimp Esquire" on the front door of your corporate office and people would just walk in and tell it to you straight, like "look, er uh Mr. Johnnie-Pimp sir, I mean Mr. Cochran, somehow I done got my ass into some shit that even OJ would say 'That *is* some shit' to, and I need you to, well, you know.......I need you to pimp me out of this!!!" Because right about now sir, you yourself are as responsible as anyone for proving that the judicial system is a playing field that can only be well maneuvered upon by the most brilliant "pimpafied" mind. You've even got black folks singing in church, "Thank the Lord for Johnnie!" It's awesome I tell you, just awesome.

Snoop Doggy Dogg

If there was a contest held today for the greatest "pimp innovator," this cat (or dog rather) would get my vote. Feel it or not, Snoop is still the all around coldest, because he's so versatile. He pimps the rap game, the film game (both kid and adult), the television game, the clothing game, the literary game, the management game, the low-key humanitarian game, he's a devoted family man and he even manufactured his own rolling papers so he could have the satisfaction of fully owning the damn joints he was smoking! I mean you can't put nothing past Snoop. I wouldn't be surprised if Mickey Mouse himself called this brotha up and said, "Yo Snoopsta, twist me up a nice one and let's talk about putting us a damn Snoopcoaster in out here at the D-house. I think they're ready for it baby."

Bill Gates

You know Bill has got this little harmless, benevolent white dude look and he almost appears sometimes like a guy who wouldn't even pimp a flea. But shiiiiit, don't let that fool you. He'll pimp that flea and yo flea bitten ass! Bill ain't about no bullshit, straight up! Bill is about pimpin' as far as the eye can see. If you go outside, take a look around you and slowly scan 360 degrees. Bill's about owning all of that. Now scan 720 degrees if you can, cause Bill's going to pimp that up too. I personally think he's from another dimension. A dimension where he already pimped everything up there, so they sent him to this dimension to come and pimp our stuff up too. He ought to change the name from Microsoft to "Microsop!" Cause he's soppin up all the damn money. And by the way, my Windows system ain't working right. Can you send a technician?

Sean "P. Diddy" Combs

Somebody sound the damn trumpets already! This pimped out brotha has arrived on top of the top of the game, and then some. Sean, look, if you wanna make a little change in the name, we're wit it. If you want us to chill on the stupid ass jokes about it, we'll chill (well, some of us will). I mean whatever you want, Mr. Combs, all you have to do is make a slight motion with yo eyebrow (just enough that one of us can pick it up) and we will get your mega-rich pimpin' ass a response ASAP. Because in a minute I'ma start calling you "Midas," Midas-Diddy, dammit! I mean the clothing line is sweet bra, but by the time you got me grooving so hard to your lil' simple-ass rapping, with all these notorious mic-slingers on the scene, I'm thinking that you might as well just go on and bust with the cane in yo funky new Sean John line, Mr. Playa Extraordinaire.

Denzel Washington

I'm telling you now, if Denzel puts on a big pimp ring, there will be you-know-whats lined up across the city waiting for a chance to get down and kiss it. That's how crazy he's drivin' 'em. Denzel pimps with an uncanny, unequaled type of charisma. Now are you trying to tell me this cat's not a magician? And to top it all off, he just plays it all off, and goes about his business of being the best and taking care of his family. So that's it ladies. There's no ring for you to kiss. Now scatter yourselves! And furthermore, you folks at the Academy better had gave him his Oscar or black people were going to start getting too tired of all the bullshit and come down there and start actin' up for a minute. You see he had to switch up and play that pimpin' ass cop role for y'all to see what was up. Now that's back to the premise of this whole book. You see what I mean? He finally got his Oscar by being the pimp that he is!

The 2003 Ghetto Famous Pimp Gallery

Ice Cube

Now picture this – you're driving down the street one day and you look up in the sky and see a blimp that reads "Cube's a Pimp." Well, like it or not, the sky ain't going no where. The sky's the limit baby! And that's just the level Cube will continue to pimp it to. He's just got too much game for the average little hateful ho out here. From the streets of L.A. to a desert storm out in who-knows-where, this ingenious pioneer west coast pimp is leaving a trail that brothas and sistas should be following and learning from for years to come. Man your setup is so cold, it only ends up being an exercise in utter self-delusion for those who are out there waiting for it to thaw. In fact, I might have to take a two-week vacation to the north pole myself, just so I can comeback all iced up and try and put it down like you, sir.

Will the Real Pimps and Hos Please Stand Up!

Malcolm X

That's right, I've got Malcolm in the pimp gallery, baby. Because nobody's put it down like Malcolm, period! And as much growth and transformation as he was going through, Malcolm was still putting it down as hard as it could be put! Because he had that pimp essence in him. Listen to me now. Malcolm knew the operative dynamics of the pimp's world from the streets first hand! That's why they were afraid of him. Because the same manipulative, misdirecting, double-talking magicianship they used to confuse and mislead the average downtrodden system-whopped ho didn't work on Malcolm. He busted their little conniving, ignorant, bigoted, crooked-tongued Whodini asses right on down. And they knew that if Malcolm was coming, invited or not, it would be a different party, straight up! Jokes aside, Malcolm is our royalty now and always. So the picture stays!!

Lil' Kim

Er uh... excuse me baby, shouldn't you be in the *other* gallery? There must have been an oversight on the printer's part, some might think. And yet the truth is, y'all know that Kim is pimpin' quite hard wit her little bold sef. She's pimpin' and hoin'. She'a pimp-ho! Naw, I'm just trippin'. The truth is, after considering other female candidates, I chose Kim because she is who she is. And she *must* be respected in the game because Kim comes off in her field, regardless. People like to joke about her, but then they turn around and market right off her talent and popularity, and groove to her music. She'll always be respected in the streets. She too gives it to ya straight, no chaser. Kim baby, we're proud of you. You just keep calling those shots and let the haters do their dance from outside the fence, Miss Queen Bee (tho a hex on the whole family!)

Samuel L. Jackson

Sam is brilliant, versatile and wild, all out here hittin' fools with golf clubs and what have you. He's pimpin Hollywood so tough, he comes out in an authentic pimp role about every two years or so, just to let us know. And in between that, he plays all the diverse intellectual cats, or action figures. And even though he was brilliant in the mathematician role he played in "Sphere," I still just got to be honest – don't Sam look just like a pimp?! (Remember he played that pimp-ass cop "Shaft." "It's my duty to please the booty!") I mean Sam, are you sure you ain't did no real pimpin' before you was acting? Cause I ran into this ho on the street the other day, and she told me she remembers working for a guy years back that looked kinda like you. Naaaw, it's probably just a coincidence. I should'na even brought it up. Keep them box office hits coming baby.

The 2003 Ghetto-Famous Pimp Gallery

Heaven

Ghetto Section

Tupac Shakur

They call Pac "the rose that grew from the concrete." And he was hands down the most quintessential young, visionary, artistic prototype, indigenous ghetto-celebrated pimp of this era. I'm telling ya Pac was about to basically pimp this whole matrix when his earthly dreamwalkin' was cut short. Still no one can take his spot in the Pimp Gallery. He had that something special, kind of like Malcolm, it was. Man brotha, where did you come from to be able to put it down like that? It will certainly take us a minute to catch back up to where you were taking us. But thank you very much for the pimping lessons anyway.

Bishop Don Magic Juan

Obviously the Bishop brings a great deal of authenticity to the gallery. I cannot even speak of him in the same light as others, because it's plainly a matter of respect. He's the Bishop. But I can tell you this – he's the wildest bishop you'll ever see in your entire life! If Isaac Newton had dropped the apple around the Bishop, it probably would have went sideways. Because the bishop has created his own gravity! And it's the most uncanny thing. His mother says he's always been that way, so it's like some kind of cosmic phenomenon. And the cosmic color-code according to the Bishop is, "I keep it green for the money and yellow for the honey!" So rookies take note.

E. Raymond Brown

Well if it ain't ol' E. Ray, the "Modern Aboriginal Gourmet Ghetto Intellectual" himself. I mean hey, I created the pimp gallery, so of course I went on and put myself in it. But let's not over-twist it baby. Unlike the others in the gallery, I have only just begun to put it down. So just prepare yourself for some ol' new type a conversation. One.

Supporting Pimps

This group is at the same level as the first team, but there's only so much room in one book, so I had to choose. My team of artists thoroughly put it down, but I've still got some acknowledging to do. So here it is peeps...

Russell Simmons - I should be ho-slapped for not having a picture of this cat in the gallery. He's put down the very pimp foundation of hip-hop music. Russell just keeps taking it to the next level, year-in and year-out. He seems to have accepted his fate of being a wise and fatherly guide to the hip-hop community. Russell could open an elite school of pimping. From fashion, to music to comedy to poetry he could easily design the ultimate curriculum.

Berry Gordy - Now here's one of the coldest most clever pimps of any period in American history. I looked up pimping the encyclopedia and saw Berry in a cold frontal shot. And let me tell you as long as there's American music playing anywhere around globe, there will continue to be a mortal Motown sound in this universe that was all possible from Berry's pimpin'.

Madonna - I remember when she first broke out with that song "Like a Virgin." People were like "Come on now, that ho ain't no virgin!" But it didn't matter. The song went to the top. And that's where this royal risqué pimp-queen puts it down from. She's all business before pleasure, or pleasure within the art within the business, or whatever her wild formula is. She's Madonna and she's running the show, and them tickets is gonna cost ya, fa sho!

Percy "Master P" Miller - Master P = Southern fried pimp mastery. This gold mouthed, rap game bangin', rodeo, whoodeehooo pimpin' ass ghetto general ain't no joke. Even if he doesn't always make the tightest moves, he makes so many tight ones, they'll far outlast the others in the conversation. Hell, he's got Wall Street businessmen taking notes on his pimping. Ga'on Perce!

Prince - This cat almost turned everybody into a ho with funky ass cuts like "Erotic City." He sho will make you do yo dance! (You know the one). Plus, he keeps the wardrobe and hairdo flyer than a hundred geese, twenty rich hos, five Chinese kites and a peacock sippin' pear tea. Every note has to be precisely stroked for you to qualify your way on stage with this Minneapolis mackster.

Suge Knight - A lot of people are intimidated by this shrewd, calculated, classic mobster vibe projectin', pimp-mogul. And as well they should pay attention to their steps around big Shuggy. Because he's just being himself – a brotha who's a product of an urban ghetto environment. You wouldn't run through a pitbull's yard actin' all stupid, so just know what you're doing in Shug's or don't be in it. For no matter what, no one can deny that he built one of the biggest west coast empires in the entrepreneurial history of black America. And he's no where even close to the mobster that George Bush is. Yet Bush is our president – so what's up with that?

Eddie Griffin - I included Eddie because he doesn't give a damn. He creates his own reality, and says whatever the hell he wants to say. He's an undercover, overcover, through your cover, blew your cover brotha. If you try and front on Eddie when he gets the mic, you're in trouble. Because he will put it down if it hasn't been put yet.

Steve Harvey - Speaking of not giving a damn about what anybody says about him, we now have Mr. Harvey as a full-timer here on the west coast. His radio show is on top of the game because of his unretracted game. He's coming at you from several angles- he's a big Hollywood personality, a strong community voice, a clown/trickster, a family man, a down to earth country-ass brotha and a leader. He's an old-school pimp who still has values. Thank God somebody's puttin' it down who does!

Jay-Z - Jiiiiiiiigga......now that's a pimped-out nick name if I *ever* heard one. And here's another brother that should certainly have a picture in the gallery. There's just no tellin' where this will all go for Jay. There's just no end in sight on the horizon of his pimpin'. It's literally his world.... And I'm just a ho-ass squirrel, about to come up on a few pimp-nuggets myself.

Missy "Misdemeanor" Elliot - She not only has you shook, Missy keeps you shook! Just so you'll know who's the pimp, baby! She runs the company, produces the tracks and drops a verse when it's all cooked up and marinated with her special hot chocolate flavored sweet buttah. Umm, ready to serve.

The 2003 Ghetto-Famous Pimp Gallery

Michael Jackson - This brother is barely hanging on to his spot in *any* gallery, the way his existential course has been taking him lately. Now hands down, no one has put it down in the entertainment business like Michael. Yet he just can't figure out how to be the pimp that he has always had the capacity to be. He needs to just forget about the aesthetics, cause he already tripped out on that. His mug looks like a cross between a China doll and a po' ho on skid row with her nose kicked off! So he might as well just pimp it from right there, or break with the full mask on 'em.

Dr. Dre - Finally Mr. Dre got his due at the Grammy's. Though everybody knows, it had already been put down years before. Dre is the west coast's big "can't stop, won't stopper." He gave over all his share of Death Row to Mr. Knight, walked away clean, and then turned around and re-pimped the whole damn thing back on an even tighter level. And now his great white hope is filling up all of his accounts. So you do the aftermath!

Eminem – At first, this little white kid had annoyed the shit out of me, I must admit. But he does make you check yourself. Because if you're hating, then you need to do some serious self-exploration above all, anyway. In the end, you will give it up – the white boy is tight! And the more he finds his own true inner pimp, the tougher he's gonna put it down on everybody.

Ice T - I wish I had this brotha as a consultant for this project, because he's more or less a walking pimp almanac! He should have been in the pictorial gallery, but with all that he keeps crackin' he ain't hardly missing nothin'. Cause it's certainly all about the *art* of pimping for Ice. With his own natural flava, he keeps it always real, versatile, fully pimped out and refreshingly sensible.

Quincy Jones - Anytime people just refer to you as "Q" it's probably because you're pimpin'. But when Q is short for Quincy Jones, then you're definitely doing some heavy weight pimpin'. Quince basically does what he wants to do, unless of course you've got more cheese than Chuckee. Then maybe he might do a little something for ya. Maybe he'll give you a little coaching and help you get a nice little Grammy or a nomination for yourself. Cause Q's got enough Grammys to hold a Grammy garage sale. And still be stuck with a pile of 'em afterwards.

Suzanne dePasse - Miss Suzanne comes from way back in the day when she was the sorcerer's apprentice, the prime minister of pimping's right hand. And so what else would she know but to put it down in grand fashion. She's hit so many homeruns in entertainment, I'm not sure whether Barry Bonds is chasing her numbers or the other way around.

Shaq - Shaq Deezy's distinction is being the biggest damn pimp on the scene. Shaq's so big, he turned around in the post to shoot a short bankshot and accidentally slam dunked the shit on three fools, knockin' em to the floor from sheer thrust. His salary alone is almost enough to buy a damn franchise. And now that his wisdom has grown to match his physical stature, he continually proves that he can put it down three-peatedly.

Clive Davis - Speaking of an active "pimpasaur," they could call this cat Pimpasaurus Rex! I mean for real, still rolling in 2003. He could just borrow Dre's chronic beat and say "Still hittin' them conas, still pimpin' them Grammys, still schoolin' the industry, still....making these hos out here recognize!" As smooth as this monsterpreneur's game is, it makes me wonder if his name ain't really "Clyde," and he's part brotha.

Earvin "Magic" Johnson - Back in his NBA heyday, on the court Earvin was indisputably the biggest pimp in the league. But even by his own admission, off the court he was the biggest ho in the league. And a fate that probably would have meant sure doom for the average one of us, only set the stage for his next great feat. For no one would have predicted that Earvin would be able to pull off pimp-slaping the aids virus like it's no more than a nagging little hoish flu germ. But he has! He might even be healthier today than he was before he contracted it. And on top of that he's slam dunkin' multi-million dollar deals like it ain't nothin'. I don't know about you, but the shit amazes me.

Michael Jordan - Let's start with this unusual stat – approximately 1,000,000,000 sneakers sold. What in the hell is so special about Mike's feet? I tell you what – they're going over yo ass, that's what! At the lengthened height of Mike's career, defenders were almost insignificant. And it has gone the same way in business. From underwear to cologne to sunglasses to long distance service to grubbin on a damn hotdog, kickin' it with Bugs Bunny, and swiggin' up on some Gatorade, Mike just sets the standard. Oop, he just scored another bucket. Yo ball out.

Suggested Pimps

This bunch was compiled from the suggestions of various individuals I randomly surveyed. I just wanted the reader to know what some of the public's perception looks like. Perhaps you have some strong suggestions or opinions of your own. Sometimes it makes for more interesting discussion to compare your perceptions with others.

Spike Lee	Will Smith
Hillary Clinton	Steven Spielberg
Michael Eisner	Dick Clark
Joe Jackson	Chris Rock
Tom Joyner	Bill Cosby
Elizabeth Taylor	LA Reid
Tracy Edmonds	Queen Latifah
Susan Taylor	Michael Ovitz
Janet Jackson	Steve Jobs
Don Cornelius	Naomi Campbell
Donnatella Versace	Earl Graves
Jennifer Lopez	The Pope
Trent Lott	Robert Johnson

Venus, Serena and they Daddy
Sanny Claus (ho, ho, ho, now you owe, owe, owe!)

I would have included Al Sharpton and Jesse Jackson but they would probably boycott the damn book!

Keepin' the Pimpin' in Perspective

Now please people, let's keep the gallery in perspective. This is not necessarily an exercise in synchronicity and agreement. It is simply a group of individuals I have chosen that represent one basic, central idea – pimping! That you may not agree or wonder how come 'so and so' wasn't mentioned, is cool. Mention them yo self, since you're all stirred up and in the mode of puttin' it down anyway.

Because I'm sure you noticed that almost all of those named were from the entertainment field, and we know that pimpin' extends far beyond that. If I were to drive down a street full of luxury homes in Beverly Hills, I'm sure there would be some famous personality living on every block. But who in the hell would own the other houses? That's the $64 question. And I've got a $65 answer – the unknown elite "nuts and bolts" pimps of America, that's who. The cats that manufacture your breakfast cereal, toilet paper moguls, auto and computer parts hustlers, professional sports team owners, fat pocketed immigrants, big-time real estate slingas, and old slavery money hangin'-out-at-the-country club ass white folks.

And sure, I could research and name a few, but they wouldn't enhance my gallery with they dry personality asses. So that's why they're not in it. But as long as we know and acknowledge all the pimpin' that's going on out here, we can keep it all in perspective – know what I'm sayin'?

*"I don't just make waves-
I am the wave."*
Don King

Onward...

We All Have a Dream, So Give a Pimp and a Ho
Room to Grow

Chapter IV

Uncle Sam Wants *You* To Come Get Some of This Good Pimpin'!!!

Chapter IV

We All Have a Dream, So Give a Pimp and a Ho Room To Grow!

"We need not approach the world from preoccupation with thoughts and feelings about being good or bad, judging whether the world is good or bad enough for us. We can just as easily live out of being fascinated with the game of creation."

Brad Blanton, Ph.D - "Radical Honesty"

    I just coincidently happened to be out here in Beverly Hills as I'm starting this chapter. And to be honest, it's not like I'm putting it down out here "on the regular," or anything like that. I just happened to be out here picking up a package for a business associate. And no, if you're speculating, it's not drug related, thank you.
    But honestly, if you don't live around here, then one thing about Beverly Hills is that it strikes out at you. These white folks out here are pimping for real! I mean sure, there's a gang of Iranians out here, and some Asians and whoever else. There are even a couple of brothas and sistas sprinkled lightly (very lightly that is) here and there.
    But come on. White folks put this joint down years and years ago, and it is a testament to what a group of pimps can get down and accomplish. My internal ho-sensor is on high alert, because I know that these white folks don't

play with your ass around here. Still, you've got to step up and represent. There ain't no more Stepen Fetchit shit jumping off. Black people aren't interested in playing your ho, in that form at least, anymore.

See we fooled around the last forty years or so and got a taste of what real big time pimping in America is like. *So we're actually looking to make this as much our dreaming as white folks have made it theirs.* We just don't plan to step on any group's humanity, or misuse it to the fullest like they've done to our own, or the indigenous Americans.

I can actually see a Beverly Hills that looks much different coming about. And I don't care if someone else sees it as hardly even a remote possibility, or if everyone knows that white folks will only let that happen over their dead bodies. I'm just another one of these new generations of African-Americans who only has one basic agenda- taking it to the next level!

So my psycho-political canvas is one where anything is possible (obviously). And not only my own people, but also many people who are champions of human rights have had to do some incredibly heavy humanitarian pimping on many fronts to create such a canvas.

Because you see, whether I show up as a pimp or a ho, in any given context from day to day, or moment to moment, I'm still going to be like Martin in the sense that I'm up in here dreaming for real. *And regardless of whether my impulse is to pimp or ho, the reality is, I've got to have some room so I can grow.*

Now if I'm the only one that's going to give it to myself, or you're the only one that's going to give it to yourself, then so be it. But hopefully, more and more as a society, we will begin to have a collective vision that views this whole universal plot as an expanding one.

I mean hey, if you've been pimping hard and heavy for the last few years, or decades, or even centuries, then you obviously have it down pat, and that's not going to change. Your internal pimping instincts heavily require that you follow them out. Trying to start a humanitarian or future development conversation with a pimp, while at the same time asking him/her not to pimp, isn't going to work.

The request instead is that one expands one's vision of pimping. It's not at all unreasonable or so outrageous to be asked to do such. For this world is turning and evolving everyday, every moment at such a rate that no one knows exactly where it's going.

Yeah, pimps are putting down the game at unprecedented levels, and with technological access that they've never pimped with before. And yes too, the degenerate "new world pimp order" is in full effect. But still, we should all consider giving ourselves a little more room to grow, to expand.

Because what the old pimps must awaken to is that there are some new pimps who will emerge, ***and these cats will put down the game from a direction that the old pimps know not.*** They will put down a new game on their old asses! A game that has only been hinted at by some of the most prophetic voices of the past and present.

The new game is going to be so deep, I can hardly even call it. It'll be so heavy, I almost don't even know what the hell I'm talking about. But it's not about me. The evolution of pimping waits for no ho, believe me.

Look for cats like Sean Combs and Percy "Master P." Miller, Ice Cube and whoever else. Then throw in

We All Have a Dream, So Give a Pimp and a Ho Room to Grow

Johnnie Cochran on the paperwork. Because Johnnie might be getting a little old, but he's still got some new vision for ya, believe me. Now imagine these savvy hood-reared pimps getting together with some of these brilliant, still open-minded, little pimpin' ass white kids, and even some of these little Asian computer-loving, technology reared brainiacs.

You know these white kids and Asians are out here buying more Snoop Dogg, and Wu-Tang than brothas. ***Hell, you've got to put them down!*** Create the conversation!...Stop bullshittin! (I'm sorry, I get a little excited).

Look, you know it's already in effect. I obviously don't even know these people. ***But I do know that they're hooking up with each other.*** And it's beyond who I can name. It's beyond who you can name. You can laugh if you want (long as you pay for a copy of this book), but I'm trying to tell you what's really cracking.

The big pimps of the world, no matter how grand their game, should give themselves room to grow too. For in a sense they're in the same boat as the rest of us. I mean surely they have deluxe luxury cabins, while most of us barely have a paddle to row with, if such an analogy is even workable. ***But they may be subtly or even out right trapped into a way of viewing all of this that even has them stuck.*** Luxury is no automatic barrier against cosmic stagnation (i.e. psychological, social and spiritual).

Any pimp can stagnate, no matter what their level. Because the cosmic order of all this is dynamic, not static. It is a constant flux and there's always new information that reveals greater and deeper aspects of the universe. We are in fact being bombarded with this new information at a rate much faster than any other time in the history of our whole evolution. Such information changes what we thought *was* so real and true, and alters how we show up in our new place of discovery. In other words, *you can become internally pimped by your own outdated way of viewing things*, and as well your own played out approaches to pimping itself!

You see, now it's not just so simple anymore. It may have once been so, but now the game is being revealed to be much more intricate and complex. So here it is not to make anything but a request. For no one knows what events will catalyze a shift in our collective psyche before it happens, or to what degree.

Now the more average pimp like you and me, or possibly like you and me *could be* if we could just stop hoing for a second, definitely needs room to grow. We need room to figure this whole thing out, or better yet, *re-figure it.* It is certainly the case for us that the requirements for pimping have increased. This is the information age for real. So you have to be continually either "staying up on game," or tip-toeing up on some way to "come up on game." The average pimp sure can't afford to stagnate, or you'll fool around and pimp your way right out of the game.

Because you have to have some room in this collective dream to grow. Being superficial won't work anymore. Maybe in the past you might have had a tight little game just making some nice money, driving your Cadillac, Benz or Lexus around, and putting in a couple of plants and a little dimmer on your living room light. But now your status has slipped off. And the bills have steadily increased along with the technological requirements for modern pimping. So you know that you have to pay for the newest PC upgrades *every year,* an expensive cellular "mackin" habit, and a DSL, *just so you can even be in the conversation, much less pimp it.*

And to top it off, people just want more, hoing or not. Your little bling-bling ain't always making the impression you hoped it would. Your dates now want more quality time, and would rather you come up with some *better quality lines!* Then your budget either cuts down on the playtime, or you can't find anyone who really wants to play when you've finally *got some time.* Your fingernails are probably growing faster than your conversation is. And your attention span is shrinking to the point to where you get sleepier than a big-eared dog when new information requires you to think on it for more than fifteen minutes at a time.

You've got to grow a little pimp, and you need room. If people could only understand that a brotha, sista, white person, Latino, Asian or whoever in this country needs room to grow and spread his or her wings so they can soar at pimping. For America is only as great a nation of pimps together as each individual pimp which comprises her. And since America's always pimpin' patriotism, she needs to be a little more patriotic herself to some of these "new jacks" out here.

Because we can't afford to have pimps out here just struggling so doggone hard. How are we going to compete with the world and stay ahead? Hell, we look out at the periphery and see the Japanese, and whoever else is trying to come up and outpimp us.

So we've got to boost the G.N.P. That's right, the *Gross National Pimping!* We've got a lot of brilliant young visionaries out here who just need a little boost in the form of a loan or something. We've got banks giving all these college kids and trade students out here all these guaranteed student loans. What about some guaranteed pimping loans?

Because you got these people coming out of college with all kinds of bachelors and masters degrees, and PhD's. And most have been educated in these large institutions run by these big time, old school academia pimps. Yet a great deal of them come out after having spent all that time and money as nothing more than an educated ho!

And like I say, there's nothing whatsoever wrong with hoing. But the fact is, within most of these young fertile ho minds, is the seed of a full and wonderful pimp, just waiting to sprout and blossom. But it needs room, water and lots of sunshine.

Unfortunately we've been so conditioned by our past experiences with so many degenerative pimp types, that our minds have become hateful and bitter. We should be giving our pimpselves room to grow and expand multi-dimensionally, yet we've become such bitter hos at times. ***Pimp hate isn't helping our evolution.*** Scoffing at a worthwhile literary contribution such as this isn't helping either!

The pimp and the ho are both divine shadow archetypes, but they have had to evolve through their adversity ridden, often socially destructive paths. Now so many, for sure, ain't worth a damn. But this dream that life is inherently involves certain core mythic roles, whether we like it and agree with it, or not.

Ask yourself who created the pimp and the ho? (Or whore, if you want to be etymologically specific). No one! That's the answer. No one except the universe, itself. They are part and parcel of an eternal plot. They

We All Have a Dream, So Give a Pimp and a Ho Room to Grow

are originated out of our living, psychic "internet" or web. They are our collective social "dreamings." *They are you and me.*

If we could just stop indicting hos for just a second, long enough to see that just because they're hoing, it doesn't mean there's no possibility of growing, it would create a shift in the world. Hos, like kids, are people too! And that would be a beautiful thing, as crazy as it may seem, to see people helping people, and hos sharing with other hos, instead of them scheming against one another and ruthlessly competing.

I mean hey, you got people all out at significant historical moments like the millennial new year or after 9-11, holding up candles, and wishing and praying for world peace. And I'm all with that. *But who do you think must be included in that wish, that prayer? Just the nice and "respectable" folk?* Hell, that category gets narrower every time someone goes out and leaves their closet open accidentally, or it just bursts from sheer build-up! You've got to include all these hos out here, and these doggone pimps in your vision of a new society.

Because the fact is, if you create a space for people to grow, then they will. I don't mean a geometric space. I'm talking about a collective expectation and supportive "holding." Just like the powerful holding of an idea that you generate within your psyche for whatever possibility to come about. These hos out here can and will grow if we as a society choose to dream that space. *Other than that, our pledges are somewhat of a farce.* Hoing has come too far as a culture, and it's too widespread.

Hos do not really have too many folks who are out there championing their cause. As a matter of fact, "ho's rights" is by nature, not much of a platform. I mean not if

Will the Real Pimps and Hos Please Stand Up!

you're going to be straight out about it. On the other hand if you want to talk about civil rights, women's rights, gay rights, rights for the homeless, or undocumented worker's rights, then you may be able to work that angle.

But the reality is that once someone begins to champion one of these causes, he or she of course becomes shifted into a pimp of some form or another, because now its about puttin' the game down. And so the cosmic cycle rolls on. *Pimps and hos are ultimately woven into one another in this life, so what can you do?* Support them both. We all dream together anyway.

Chapter V

This is a similarity of the symbol that's printed on the back of the U.S. one dollar bill. The thing for you to know is that it's a pimp symbol, straight up.

The breakdown goes like this; the eye at the top of the pyramid represents the "ultimate, super-rich degenerate, global power pimp group." It is made up of a small group of individuals who control incredible sums of wealth that the average ho cannot possibly fathom. What do the bricks in the pyramid represent, you wonder? (Even if you don't wonder, I'm telling you). They are all structural pieces in their "new world pimp order." Owners of multinational corporations and global banking are the biggest bricks nearest to the top. Powerful masons, presidents and the corrupt leaders of nations are the bricks underneath them. Between them and the bottom layer are all the rest of the scrambling pimps and conniving little hos of this "rat race" that will get in wherever they can fit in, believe me. And oh yes, the bottom layer....why that's you and me, playa. Your play.

Chapter V

The Plot Only Gets Thicker

In the most recent year for which there are figures, forty-four of the top eighty-two companies in the United States did not pay the standard rate of 35 percent in taxes that corporations are expected to pay. In fact, 17 percent of them paid NO taxes at all- and seven of those, including General Motors, played the tax code like a harp, juggling business expenses and tax credits until the government actually owed them millions of dollars!
   Michael Moore "Stupid White Men"

The title of this chapter presents a great truth. Because if you're still reading this book after all the bizarre and provocative content so far, then you're probably already used to it being fairly thick out here anyway.
   See, I'm not tripping, because people can easily say "come on now, all that crap he talked about the reality of pimps and hos is not the truth. The world shouldn't be viewed in such an offensive, uncouth, raw and derogatory context." And I would respond by saying, "Hey, I understand where you're coming from." I would be put off and incensed by a world full of people talking about pimps and hos all the time too. For certain, the world is vast and unlimited. And there are a billion applicable viewpoints, depending upon your position and disposition.

But what I will point out is that the world only becomes "cooked," rather than raw, and refined rather than uncouth, and neatened rather than messy, through the cultural dressing that we process and marinate our experience with.

And thank God we know how to do this. I would shudder to try and imagine what a society would be like of communicators who are just absolutely raw all the time. Our experience as humans is much more pleasant with a bunch of coats of descriptive cultural primer, paint and varnish. It's what creates its richness. And this is an outcome of our core ability and nature to dream together. This *is*, in fact, our dreaming. And I understand fully that there is nothing as important to any group as it's dreaming.

But in that same whole context of "dreaming," is the importance of downright existential authenticity. The all out dissection, exploration, confrontation and rediscovery of each layer, each brush stroke, each fiber and each thread which makes up the whole is just as valid, necessary and contributive.

Sure, I have joked a lot, but the truth is that the world of the pimp is the world of power. The pimp puts it down, bottom line. The world of the ho is focused around an available love, receiving what is put down, and the service of such. A ho can be anyone in a sense. All she or he has to do is follow and serve the program. True enough, we should note, the wisest, most insightful pimp minds have started with such a humble foundation (the Taoists say that the wisest leader is one who knows how to follow).

Yet when I'm in certain awesome meditative spaces or out in nature, I don't have to deal with any such dynamics or conversations, and for the most part I don't. But as a dweller in everyday urban cosmopolitan reality, in a rapidly changing and evolving, globally interwoven society, from the time when I wake up and go out in the morning until the time I return home and go to sleep at night, I experienced the world of the pimp, thank you. And there are plenty of hos about, including myself in so many instances, but the pimps call the overwhelming majority of shots. And that's the reality I see all these coats of primer and paint and shellac going over. And yes, I am quite capable of this articulation. I can at least pimp this much, for sure.

Because like I say, the plot's not getting any thinner. And I'm sure that that has something to do with the fact that I live in Los Angeles, the "City of the Angels." Because if this is a city full of angels, then there are certainly a great variety of those here, for real! And that would mean that there also are some angelic pimps and hos.

Pimps generally like their plots thicker. They like to be in the "thick of things," putting it down. Some of the biggest pimps today are superb multi-taskers. Yet because they don't do most of the footwork, you could say that they're great "multi-focusers." The more that things go down around them, the more you can rest assured that they're putting down. Thus in a world in which the wheels will hardly cease to turn, the pimp is utterly content in the plot. Most pimps are not talking about slowing the game of life down one iota.

Hos on the other hand, can certainly "exist" in the thick of things, ***but they usually run somewhat thin.*** While the wheels of the modern world are spinning forth seemingly uncontrollably, the average ho is merely just trying to hang on to a spoke or two, and keep that ass from dragging too close to the ground. He or she is just existentially "out here" in the system, trying to "do what I gotta do" to somehow make it by.

You've got to love the ho because the ho has, and demonstrates spirit, if nothing else. The ho is going to just somehow get her/his task done, and then get the hell out of there and have some real fun as soon as she/he gets a chance. A ho may not be able to figure out the whole plot, but she sure as hell loves to play, no matter what. The pimp is also playful, but he or she obviously plays in a different dynamic having put down the game in the first place.

As the world evolves and becomes more and more complex through technological advancement, pimping as a whole only increases in its sophistication. Uncle Sam has come a long way from the days of fooling around with a group of broke ass pilgrims. ***The U.S. government is now focusing on a new frontier of imperialism- space!*** The "colonization" of space is at the top of the agenda.

Now that surely is a conversation that's beyond the conception of most. But in fact, the program is being put down right now, as we ho. You see, what the average everyday layho may view as nothing but abstract empty space millions of miles from our planet, the top pimp-scientist minds working for our government view as an incredibly useful, advantageous and new form of ho. They view outer space as a new territorial "promised land" that will work totally for them.

While you and I don't even have time for such a conversation, they already have the technology up there to spot the dry outer layer of skin on your ass that you need to get a loofah and scrub off! And you didn't think anybody saw that shit!

Why from space they can watch, control and manipulate almost everything. So where do you think your ho ass is going? Do you think that these pimps don't mean business? The fact is after World War II, a great many officers from the S.S., Hitler's high command, escaped to the United States and a few moved into top positions in the U.S. space program. So these crazy ass pimps are out here taking it to the next level, with Lil' Georgie's little Eddie Munster looking-ass, and they're pimping you, the tax paying ho, for trillions of dollars to fund this "out-of-space" campaign. Thickness indeed!

But it only gets thicker. They say the gap between the rich and the poor is widening. About less than one half of one percent of the population presently controls more wealth than the bottom fifty percent combined. *So they might as well say that that gap is forever widening*, because I've been hearing the same damn thing ever since I could distinguish a statement in the English language!

Of course it gets wider. What do you think they would do, say, "Hey, why don't we do less pimping this year? Let the hos catch up a little." They'll keep widening the gap until it's wider than the pacific. But all the while they're widening the gap, they'll be quietly moving right up on your ass, and moving you right on over.

They'll put a block of deluxe luxury condos smack dab in the middle of some homeless shanty town, just because some big, ruthless, bottom-lining developer says "never mind over there, this'll work right here!" And all the homeless people will get as compensation will be two soup cans, a half a pack of cigarettes and a new cardboard box. And a few of their broke asses ull' be out there lapping up that soup, smokin' a square, talking about "hmmm, this is a pretty cool box."

If you don't believe me, then go to downtown Los Angeles. Do you know that there are people that come from other parts of the world, other societies, and they don't believe this! *They wonder how in the hell do you have a city the size of Los Angeles, with all the money we have, and you can still have this big of a homeless population.* It doesn't make any sense to them.

But it makes sense to us Angelinos. Or all of us "angels," that is. We understand it perfectly. Pioneer rap artists Run DMC put it succinctly- "It's like that, and that's the way it is, huhhh!!!" But then not everyone listens to rap. At least not DMC's rap. However, here they do listen to the unwritten everlasting rap-code of inner city pimping. It goes "the rich get richer, while the poor get poorer," or even further translated *"the pimp get pimper, while the ho get hoer!"*

Ya know, a famous poet once wrote, "the thickness runs through my psyche's veins, as I experience how utterly pawnish I feel in this great game." Now of course he may not be famous to you, but he is to me- I wrote it! *And I'm telling you the game is so thick, I can hardly see myself out here!*

Take the real estate game for example. I could, of course, talk about the stock market, the pharmaceutical industry, the media or the insurance game. But each one of those in itself would be about half a book on pimping alone. So let's just take a quick glance at real estate.

I remember when as a kid, my dad first explained to me about a mortgage and the principle, and how when people rent, they pay every month and don't even own a thing. I thought to myself, "Wow, how could someone commit to giving someone else money every month, while the other person owns everything?" I mean I used to play monopoly a lot. And it got crazy, especially playing with some of my relatives. But never that crazy! I just didn't get it.

But now I do. I know some people with very nice apartments, very sufficient incomes, and stable employment, but yet they still feel they're just not interested in buying. I like everyone else, pretty much understand that *really anyone would want to buy if they could, or if they saw that they could buy as advantageously as they could rent.*

But buying real estate is a big conversation. It's hardly an impossible one. But if you ever go to a real estate seminar, you realize that there are an important group of distinctions that you must know. And if you have any friends who are real estate professionals, then you hear them talking the jargon all the time- reverse mortgage, interest only loans, liquidated damages, P.M.I. (not to be confused with P.M.S.).

They seem hardened, no matter how wonderful they are. And it's not because they are successful or unsuccessful. *It's that being involved in the real estate game has had them develop a hardened outer coating. And that's because it's a straight up and down pimp's game, period!*

So much so, that even people who dib dabble at a relatively small level (with some success) feel more "pimpish," the more they pull off owning. All you have to do is listen to them talk about their properties. They talk about them like they are their hos. They may be proud, happy "first time" pimps or owners. But their happiness at such a small level in the game gives them away. For once they get into that note a few months, then years, ***they know that real estate is a big pimps game, indeed!*** At a smaller level you feel pimpish, but not that pimpish.

Because now your eyes have opened and you see the light. The light I'm talking about is the one that's directed on the concept of the big game board. Just think about it. ***Why is it that most people will never own? Ever!!*** Go sit up in a seminar full of first time buyers, or even just listen in on a conversation with some. You may notice, if you watch carefully, that all of the terminology has a draining effect upon one who is not used to dealing with it. It even drains a lot of the people who *are* used to it.

Do you think that this is purposeful, that maybe it is by design? Because it certainly wears a great many people down. The only one who is an exception to being worn down is the fat-pocketed real estate pimp. Everybody else is praying and crossing their fingers, and holding their breath, just hoping to make it through escrow. Why the truth is, most hos can't even express a working definition *of* escrow, much less make it through it. They probably think its some kind of freakin' bird or something.

And it's as pathetic as it is hilarious. It's hilariously pathetic. Because at least in being the average ho, you *can* afford a good chuckle. Other than that, the real estate game is an utterly draining conversation. ***They've got you sitting up there "thinking" about buying.... for how long? For how many years?***

Why by the time most of us decide to actually step out beyond our little ho-length radius and buy something, they'll have raised the market so high, it'll cost you about three hundred thousand dollars just to pull off a foreclosure on a crackhouse in Watts! And you'll be out there trying to slap some cheap ass paint and tile over all the crackpipe marks, so you can somehow figure out a way to turn it all over on the next wanna-be ghetto tycoon.

Finally, by the time you've become at least moderately disheartened from pouring your last savings, along with whatever you could borrow off the slowly withdrawing support from family and friends, you resolve to push through the whole ordeal and make a paltry couple of thousand or so. Such may be all part of an upcoming few-year lesson package entitled "Your First Venture into Real Estate."

But the big pimp, on the other hand, doesn't even shudder in a general real estate conversation. The only time he/she may flinch is when he attempts to possibly bite off more than he can pimp. But even still, he/she is generally able to mobilize resources.

Meanwhile, the rest of us are left to gaze at all the late night infomercials with absolutely dumbfounded curiosity. And we all pretty much have the same question– How much time and energy would I dare to risk to allow some questionable pimp named Carlton to walk me into the "valley of the shadow of realty," while taking my little hard earned ho–sum of money? The answer? Nothing ventured, nothing pimped baby! As a ho, you of course know from experience that that's the way it works. You've got it take it somewhere for sure. The only question then is, how much can you pull off the encounter for yourself? Sound familiar?

You could always consider just going to an actual real estate school and skipping the old shortcut. Of course by the time you've spent a great amount of time and energy in that, you'll still start off at the bottom basically. You'll still have to *you know what* for a while, license or not.

The Plot Only Gets Thicker

Because as a ho, it's basically *all* school! All of your experience has been a continual form of schooling. On any given day in the infinite span of this whole social plot you search for your hopefully worthwhile lesson. How can you in fact get the most for yourself, even when it's a given that you will have to take it one way or another, in one sense or another, from one pimp or another?

You don't seem to be as far as you'd have thought even when you move up in grade. And your zeal and luminosity seem to be ever leaking out with the same old program, higher mileage and age. Alas, for all your education, there is ultimately no diploma. There are only the perennial lessons of hoing.

It's a cold game I know. But don't be mad at me. I didn't bring all the ice. I just happen to be at the party. And the DJ's bumpin some vintage Snoop- "It's a Doggy Dog World." It's thickness baby, I'm telling you.

But it only gets thicker. For the ho mind is like a screen that is always bombarded with continuous images – traffic, work, dreams, nightmares, daymares, always running images. Sometimes you have moments of catching up to these images, where you feel lucid and alive. But mostly they are a continuous succession of life scenes, ever pressing forward.

The pimp, on the other hand, is like the director and the projector all in one. He/she is creating the script and projecting the film onto your ho-screen-mind. As a ho, you wake up, live in the script, and only vaguely if at all, conceive of a possibility of being able to actually make the film that is your day to day life. A ho doesn't have access to the powerful life-editing capacity of the pimp. So it becomes almost impossible to stop the succession of images, after the film has lapsed him or her far enough into unconsciousness, or should I say "ho-consciousness." Remember now, pimps are magicians at their most powerful level.

As a ho, you get to be a star. A star in your own little segment of this great film that life is. Now if you look on the daily script, you'll see your part. It's right there, by where it says ho. That's where you come in.

Are you happy? If you're happy, then the pimp's happy. Because he likes for you to be happy, and contented with your part in the film. But if you're not happy...then *possibly someone will have to think about what they can do with another unhappy ho.* Maybe you can get some ice cream or refreshment, or someone can take you for a little ride to clear your mind.

Maybe you should be told that it's all a lie, that there really are no pimps out there making your movie. It's probably just all a figment of your imagination. Something like a "fig-pimp," or a "pimpment." They are known to show up in the thickness out here.

But it only gets thicker. Particularly if you are of "higher status," whatever the hell that is. And of course I know what it is, and you know what it is. And we both know and agree which is what makes it some actually meaningful bullshit. But can anyone tell me *how is one human being truly of higher status than another?* Now if you have any freakin' sense left, then you should be able to distinguish that *"status" is the ultimate pimp's game!*

That you are from the royal family, or of a higher breed, or come from a more "favorable" family background, is a trick, straight out! And people are out here left and right looking to hang with someone who can pimp their own status a little bit more than they can, so they'll be able to view their own hungry, empty, hoish asses as somehow more valid in the world.

There are probably some people who are holding this book right now and caught up in that bullshit. But I don't mean you of course. But you know there are some status-seeking hos out there, probably no further than a hundred yards at most. And they're playing the role to the hilt, trying to come up in America. They may be the nicest people. But so many of us have basically been conditioned to hang out and associate ourselves with only the highest grade of social pimp that we can distinguish, and somehow slip up next to.

And we are so fooled by the inauthenticity of it all. For the people we hang out and associate with just for their perceived "status," usually end up being bigger and more inauthentic hos than ourselves in so many ways.

However, the pecking order continues all across American society. The people up on the hill don't usually come hang out much with the people on the bottom, anymore than the people on the west side hang out over on the east side. Any exceptions to this are usually just that, exceptions. And even though it may be subtle, it's still very present. Pimping a little higher than the next person is the American way.

Now if you look at the demographic in terms of what we in this country know as race, it becomes less subtle. White people at the top automatically know from their social and educational curriculum, or "pimpication," that seriously associating with "those hos" out there could jeopardize their whole game. So they need to make sure that there is a sophisticated system of higher pimpicational institutions that is maintained and celebrated. They need the Harvards and the Dartmouths and the Yales to be kept amply funded and pruned.

Yes, they've got to prune not only the trees, but also the student population. They've got to prune my black ass and whoever else's off the campus if too many of us start flocking that way. And being the magicians that they are, they surely have many of you fooled. They have you thinking that it's all about education, when in fact it's all about pimping.

And this is not to complain. I'm not going to sit up here and be some naggin' little, excuse making ho. But whatever role I do show up in, I'm going to be as real as I can. These magicians are not fooling me like that. I may struggle, but I'm not that baffled. You see, we can listen to the national anthem together, but I don't sing. I just hum because it's a familiar tune, and I'm right here in this dream too. *I understand that at a deeper level we all must co-compose the music of life.*

Yet I see America's little funky "pecking order." Asians get right in there as a group where they can. They'll come buy up all they can in anyone's neighborhood, because they're basically quiet and methodic pimps. They embody thousands of years of pimping wisdom, along with a sense of balance we do not understand here in this western dream. And I don't think Confucius said it, but they do seem to believe, "If white man put you in position to pimp black, brown and red American, then you must accept gift in high honor." Because they don't drop a step, let me tell you. If they can squeeze in and pimp it, it's a done deal!

Because Asians come in all complexions. *And if you go to their countries, you find out that the lighter ones pimp the darker ones, quiet as it is kept.* You see, just because this conversation is not held much, *it doesn't mean it is not to be held.* I didn't even know that there were darker complected Chinese and Japanese people until I got to college. So its nothing for Asians to come into the American socio-political pimping system and work right on in.

Now I'm of course referring to them as a group, not as individuals. Anyone of them may be one of the nicest people you'll ever know. But as a group, they'll pimp your ass the same as anybody will! But you'll have to excuse me. I'm just out here, and it's a little thick, that's all.

I checked the latest forecast of the social/political climate this morning. They said it's getting thicker. And for the next few days, it'll be cloudy and thick. Then it'll clear up and be very hot, and "thicky." I just heard a broadcast that four hos got stopped earlier at a Beverly Hills convention by security. They had to send them home, for "frontin' on their status!" But it's been another long day again, and its now sunset.

Beware of Pimp

If only the Native Americans knew or had a clue hundreds of years ago, when they looked out and saw the sun set on this great land. They saw the great mother earth and her abundant coat of nature. They saw trees sprawling forth vibrantly decorated with lush green leaves and flowers. They saw nature's children, the animals, moving about freely. There was the bear, the wolf, the squirrel, the snakes, the birds and the ho. Oh, wait a minute! They didn't see any ho. I meant *hole.* They saw the snake going into the hole.

And they also saw themselves at peace and in harmony with it all. Too bad they didn't see the thickness of the plot that was to come. Too bad they did not see the game that would be put down. And too bad they weren't able to prepare for the new dreaming called "America." Too bad they wouldn't have any network on television in this day and age to let you know their experience of what the strange pimp-like newcomer was to call "progress."

Of course we are now in the new millennium, sailing forward at one moment, smashing forward into the next, and seemingly being dragged into the next by who knows what destiny. And though it may seem as though I'm digressing by reminding us of how America has showed up for someone other than the pilgrims and the colonists, I know that the fully mirrored context of our origin only makes us more conscious. It not only makes us more conscious, and perhaps somewhat disturbed, but we are certainly made more awake.

Today I don't have to be sold from any auction block, or be chained like an animal, or "Jim hoed," I mean "Jim Crowed." I don't have to go around to the back door, unless everybody's going in that way. I can receive an education, and read and write freely. And I seem to be taking advantage of that, for real!

I can make a lot of money. And if I am able to generate it legally, or seemingly legally, like a lot of Americans, I can live a pretty incredible life. I could even run for political office if I could somehow convince enough Americans, like other candidates, **that they would be less worse off voting for me.**

So it seems like there's a momentary space of utter thinness. Like the plot is just all good and simple. You know, be good, do good, and it's gonna be all good.

Except that space of utter simplicity and thinness seems to always get interrupted. *Interrupted by the very plot itself!* Hell, what was I thinking? Just because I was over the crest of the last wave of social intensity and my daily dose of life's existential onslaught, it doesn't mean that another wave wasn't on its way! I mean I've got so much to do, and so much to catch up on, after I catch up on *what I really have to catch up on* this minute as we speak. I don't think it ends.

Then I've got some silly ass notion that my money "fantasy" will relieve it all, if and when it ever occurs. And well, it will relieve a hell of a lot, true enough. But even big pimps still have even bigger problems.

And society's not going to let up. There are more people everyday, with not only more needs, but also more wants, *and more game!* And that means more pimping! You've almost got to sleep with one eye open, because your internal pimp sensor keeps signaling, and you know that there's yet another human being out there close enough who's going to attempt to put down some type of game on you.

You'll even run into a few homeless "hustlers" every once in a while who've got the nerve to try and slip a little pimp in on you, with their utterly hoed down asses. All up at the gas station talkin' 'bout, "Yo man, gimme a dolla!" Not "Can you please...?" or "Will you...?" just "Gimme!" As if you could really stand just one more notch of the game coming your way at that moment.

And here you are out here just merely trying to help yourself, and your loved ones. But they're all going through the same thing at varying levels. So you know that you'll have to leave so much up to divine order, cause down here there's all too much of ze'pimp order cracking! And if you truly want anything, you better commence to pimping a little tougher yourself.

Just Make Sure They Know Who's Out Front!

That's why we admire the big pimps so much in this society. Because they remind us of who we are. They remind us that we've got to keep the world reminded. *Hell, you can't have any weapons if we say you can't! Never mind how many we have. We don't even know how many we have.* We've lost count. The inventory's too damn big to keep recounting!

It's so big, we can tell you, Mr. Sadam or Mr. Whoever, whatever we want to tell you. All we've got to do is get President Bush's speech writing team to write up a few fast food allegations and some quick side-order quality press releases, and by the time the American public is skillfully induced, we'll start swiping at every puff of conjecture like a kitten playing with a knat! At that point, no matter how intelligent we are as individuals, we'll all be levitated once again to our familiar state of collective mass airheadedness, mixed in with a little hyper-patriotic machismo.

But can anyone blame us? What in the hell else is there for Americans to do? *I mean come on, don't people know we're out here trying to win the human race?* And we're way out ahead, you let us tell it. Way out! We're so far out ahead in global pimping, we're about to lap ourselves just to make it more interesting!

But hold on. Coming up on the inside in lane three, are the Japanese, pimping with the latest supra-mega-fiber-multi-hydro-optic-laser-micro-mini systems on the market. Their new equipment is so high tech, they even got Japanese scientists saying to each other, "Look buddy, I'm telling you the Japanese don't even have this shit!" So you can never really count a group with such unrelenting technocracy out.

And look here on the outside lanes, four, five and six. You've got France, China and India, followed by Britain (our former pimps), Germany and a host of others.

Now the French are slick. They'll serve you some fine wine and bread. And then just when you are feeling real toasty, they'll "le'pimp" you! The Chinese will serve you up a tasty dish or two. And then they'll jam some of that eerie "gonging" music, while whispering a few ancient proverbs in your ear. And before you know it, you'll be a practicing ho with quiet legs, "like grasshoppa."

Now India is a real trip. I know they've been trying to get down with democracy, but they've actually had pimping straight up "molded" into their worldview. They've had what they call a "caste" system for over a thousand years. *That basically means your ass is "casted" into either pimping or hoing for not only one life, but possibly many lifetimes.* Can you imagine entering into your next life and saying, "Damn, you mean I got to ho again!?" Black people in America call that condition being "tow back!"

Imagine knowing that shit even before you leave your current lifetime. Your whole society saying to you, "Hey buddy look, being a ho is just your karma." I'd be saying to whoever told me first, "Buddy my ass, why do I have to be the ho? How come hoin' ain't *your* karma?" And if the person replied, "It is!" then I would say, "This all sounds too suspicious. You probably just want to make sure you keep some company down here for the next few lives. You don't want to have to ho it alone!"

And while I really don't know how all that works, I suspect some "Prince Habib" or something is pulling the ol' game. They've got some cat playing that funny lookin' clarinet. And while the snake starts coming up from the basket, it stares you in the eye, and you begin to feel..... kind of "hoish."

I mean I'll admit I'm another dumb ass American when it comes to other people's cultures. *But some of it just doesn't make sense by almost anyone's standards!* India knows they've had some of their leaders up in there running game. Look at how they've had all these potentially good pimps out there just'a starving in them streets, while all kinds of healthy fat ho-stock just strolls around free and untouched! I'm telling you most Americans just don't get it. We'd have been pimped that ho-stock, and then opened up some burger stands!

Plus the British have been over there pimping their white asses off! And America too. That's right. You probably didn't even know that ol' Enron went over there and set up power plants and then locked their government into a multi-billion dollar contract that they knew the Indians didn't have enough money to pay for. And then they were threatening to take and auction off the peoples' government buildings unless they gave them all their money. Tsk tsk tsk! You see, you can't talk about my ghetto ass, *because I see you,* you "bloody pimps!"

But the British have Lennox Lewis, their "great black hope." Now Lennox is a smooth and undisputed pimp for sure. And Americans thought that Mike Tyson would possibly get with him, but Lennox straight pimp-slapped him. That wasn't easy for some of us from the hood to watch. He treated Mike like a bitch. But that's okay, because like a true American, my man Mike got paid! So cheerio, old chap!

What about the Germans? People don't know exactly what's going on with them these days. But I'll tell you what. As long as they don't try and pull that old Nazi-Hitler crazy pimp shit off again, then we're cool. I mean I've met some German people and they were really nice, but you've got to watch they ass (and I'm not talking about the booty!).

But who else is out there? "Second world," "third world" countries. You've got Saudi Arabia, Nigeria, Australia, Israel.... Israel! Awwhhh shit. Wait a minute. You've got to slow - it - down to break it down about Israel. Because those Jews have so much pimp power in America, **they'll crucify your ass** in the paper, on the news, at the bank, and everywhere else, **for just mentioning them if they don't like you.** You'll be like Samuel L. Jackson in that movie, throwing the computer on the floor of the bank, after they get through with you. And they know it. You'll be broke, reputation all tore up in the paper, and unemployed...unless you know how to make some incense. They might have you so jacked up, people won't even buy incense from yo black ass. Your own grandma won't even let you in and feed your hungry ass, **talkin' about "How dare you say that about the chosen people!"**

I mean come on! They get down on this pimpin' thing thoroughly at all levels, and have you all twisted up. I mean how in the heck do you try to con me into believing God is choosing one group of us over another? My Pan-African studies professor told me "If God chose any of us, then he chose all of us, period!" Now that's what I'm talking about.

You can practice any religion you please, but don't come at me pimpin' other peoples' history and heritage. Eastern Europeans are not, I repeat, are not indigenous to the area now called Palestine and Israel! They are indigenous to Eastern Europe. The indigenous Jews to the Palestine/Israel area look more like me, homeboy!

And I'm not saying that you don't have a right to be there. But you certainly don't have a right to slaughter up the indigenous Palestinians and force them on to a little strip or reservation, like they did the Native Americans here. It's that simple!

Besides that, what's up with all those diamonds you've been running out of South Africa and the Congo for decades? They end up right over here on the market, and my people over there end up dead in some mine, working for you, or dead broke! I mean from one pimp to another homie, what's up with that!? *Oh shit, my lights just went out! Uh oh. They're going to have me out here looking like Will Smith in "Enemy of the State." Time to talk about another country...*

Now speaking of somebody pimping their way right out of the game, what in the hell happened to Russia? Remember how big time they were? I remember when they had everybody scared over here in America. People use to think, "Oh shit, the Kremlin might do this. The Kremlin might do that. What in the hell are we gonna do to protect ourselves from these big ol' Eastern pimps?" We thought that they might bomb us without even taking a lunch break. But they took a lunch break all right.

Little did we know that the day would come when they couldn't even afford to put some damn gas in one of the tanks, much less pay for a couple of fresh shells to shoot off. I mean how did that happen? Russia was pimping so hard! Then one day it all just melted down like an old raggedy ass nuclear reactor. Somehow their money ain't worth a hand full of dust. All of a sudden the people said, "The hell with this communist bullshit, tell us how we gonna make some money!" And they went from basically being the biggest pimps in the east, to some of the brokest, most disillusioned hos on the map. Now that's what I call a total "pimp meltdown."

To tell you the truth it just goes on and on. Australia is still pimping the Aborigines, the oldest living group. They aren't even indigenous Australians. Those are British settlers keeping them little hos broke and "outback." The Saudi's got all that oil, and keep pimpin' em real slick! The brothers over in Nigeria have got a little oil too. They've got some oil and some tight little dashiki outfits. Have you ever seen a pimp in a dashiki? It's a cold thing.

What about Mexico? Those are beautiful people, but they're getting a little tired of coming up here and selling all them oranges and stuff on the side of the freeway. The way they see it, what we call Texas, California, Arizona and New Mexico is really their land. So they're only hopping the fence into their own yard! That's why when you try to tell them some old American Yankee bullshit, they act like they don't understand your ass! But if you say "this is yours," believe me they will say "Siiiiii!" And furthermore, while you think they're so content at hoing their way along, in ever-growing numbers, they're quietly pimping their way right up on your ass.

And even the little nations like Yemen are doing their thing slangin' a little oil out the side border, talking about,

Will the Real Pimps and Hos Please Stand Up!

"How many barrels do you want? Just pull your shit around the side and park." So everybody's just mashing and trying to put it down as much as they can. That's why we can't afford to get too inflated. Well maybe we can afford it, but after September 11th reintroduced us to the idea that we're hardly the only ones who can cheat on the ol' humanitarian pledge game, we're back to focusing a little more on our own form and stride. They kinda put a pimp back on her toes a little. The old tortoise really got one off on us. He clipped both a rabbit's ears in one scratch.

So now we've got to put on some heavier platformed rabbit shoes, thicker denim jeans, and a sturdier, wider, new red, white and blue alloy brimmed hat, and get out here and start high kneeing our way back out in front of this human race.

Because we are some crazy multiple personality disorder-ass Americans. And you don't like that I call your ass crazy? How in the hell can you be the "leader of the free world" and simultaneously participating in its enslavement and exploitation everywhere?

Everywhere America's big business corporations can milk resources, labor and profit, at whoever's expense, they will milk. ***Everywhere America's government can exploit the opportunity to collaborate with oppressive regimes and get paid, they will do it!***

Yet she shifts over to this benevolent, global earth-angel faster than Sybil in a stress attack! "We're such good Americans. We want only the best for everyone. We want only what's righteous and pure." And the killer is that this side of us is sincere. This benevolent, liberty waving, tear jerking, impeccable, ethical, moral, ultra heroic, human godlike prototype doesn't have a clue to how utterly repulsive its inconcealable counterside is. And the complexity and irony of it all is such that, as individuals, we are mostly an incredibly wonderful batch of human beings.

Some of us Americans though, say "Yes we do have a clue to our collective schizophrenia." ***And these are the truly honest people, white, black, or whomever.*** But I say no, I think not. Because if America had a clue how conclusively self delusive she presents herself to any human who can really read a history book and simply observe and think from a balanced human perspective, we would just laugh like a little devious young kid caught stealing in a candy store, and cop to it. ***Yes, we would cop to it all!***

So there, I said it. The great American empress doesn't have any clothes on. She is only a naked, wealthy, manipulative, heavily armed, multiple personality disordered bully, who wants people to think she's much more mature than she truthfully is.

How dare I say this America? How dare you "how dare" me, pimp!! That's right, I called you a pimp, Mr. and Mrs. America. And I'm one of you too, like it or not. So let us be free and exercise some of these rights that people have been out here getting killed for hundreds of years, just so we can have the option of using them.

And no I'm not angry. I may be a little unnerved from time to time. Perhaps like anyone else in the midst of such thickness. But I actually like it here in America. I don't even really know anywhere else. I mean I've been places, but I don't really know them like I know America. So all I can say is, "God bless our crazy asses!"

But I don't think God is going to continually bless those pimps who put all those secretive symbols on the money. Why, we don't even know what they mean. And the pimping pace in this race is moving so fast, it doesn't even matter if someone informs us anyway. Because there are people who run our society and the global power structure who pimp on a level that is unfathomable to the average layho. They pimp on a level that is way beyond the smaller frequency of layho conversation and attention span. So you can't ever really quite figure out how the plot got so thick. You just know its thick, and you've got to somehow keep it moving.

And try raising a kid in all of this and explaining to them what the hell us adults have going on. Why, you have to be a master revealer. *Because you can't just jump into it. You have to reveal this complex, entangled, adult bullshit that exists on the global scene to them bit by bit.* Because you want to keep them encouraged, while somehow trying to bleed your own authentic disgust and ignorance into the conversation.

But by the time they're old enough to assimilate the language (at about 12 or 13), if you care to be an honest parent, you just feel like copping to it all. Particularly if you have a little African-American child, and want him or her to be up on the game. You have to say "look, we must all learn to respect the great process of life. But America is full of bullshit, sweetheart! You see that nice colorful looking Mr. Uncle Sam is nothing but a sneaky old pimp."

It's All in the Twist

Okay, so I said America is full of bullshit, straight out. But that doesn't mean I'm throwing the towel in on her by far. I'm just being honest. So don't get it twisted, even though it already is!

What I mean is don't "mistwist" what's already very twisted and paradoxical. Because if you mistwist, which basically means misinterpret, then you'll just further confuse and fluster your already over simplistic-minded ass in the middle of a very tricky and in-depth stretch of the road.

Because life is process. And process can be most paradoxical, particularly in a very large group situation. A paradox of course means that there are two truths that seemingly contradict, but somehow they don't within the greater truth. And of course you knew this already, and I know that you knew it because you are a paradox yourself, right Mr. and Mrs. American?

That you and I are both momentary and eternal, solid and fluxual, ancient and contemporary, particle and wave, individual and group, brilliant and stupid is just a given. It's just our cosmic "playing field." We all show up in this dance, and it is just that – a weird dance.

I am not you ***in one conversation,*** and then we start talking about this totally mythic creature called an "American," ***and I become you, and you become me – the American.*** You sing, "Gave proof through the night that our flag was still there," and my black ass was about to be sold for about three and half schillings or some shit the next day. I didn't know where the hell I would be, but you're singing about that flag thinking the song sounds so great and all, so I'm just watching you sing.

Because this is all a dream, remember? You call it an "American dream." But of course if I'm talking about being in a dream, then I must be crazy. Because you say I must come to grips with "reality." And reality, according to I don't know who- I guess probably the church, or the pentagon, or Freud, or the surgeon general, or Oprah Winfrey, or Deepak Chopra, or Ted Koppel (don't he look like Alfred E. Newman?) or definitely not George Bush, or I guess all of us- is not a dream. But yet it is. And we call it "America."

So it's all very twisted and paradoxical. Though most of the time, the way we've basically learned to think, things are just straight. They're just what they are. This book is a book. It's a crazy book, but that's just what it is. You're probably a little crazy too, but you don't have to let on about it to anyone. You wouldn't want to jeopardize your "status." Today is today, and tomorrow will be another day. Someone is in fact pimping this moment, as we speak, here in America. Someone is also hoing, as we speak. It's just straight up stuff that we have to deal with daily.

And our straightness keeps the plot of life clarified. We can say at any given moment, "Hey wait, let me get this straight." And you're a thankful human being when you get it straight. Because *seeing* the plot is important. No one wants to live in murkiness all the time.

But no matter how straight you're getting it, somehow life always seems to throw you a curve, a twist. And bam, there it is. That old twist again. And before you can untwist that one and get everything back straight, bam! Another twist! And then while you're bent over, looking over there and working on that, bam! Two more from the other direction. *And pretty soon life is just life again, full of twists.* And the plot just thickens most surely on your ass...and on all of us.

For instance, yeah, I talked a lot of crap, but I don't make the world the way it is. We all make it the way it is together! So just because it's all twisted up, it doesn't mean it's time to bail out. No siree. On the contrary, we have to grow deeper into the riddles and the twists.

We've got all kinds of pimps and hos out here. We've got pimps who are out here pimping hos, while some hos are out here trying to pimp other hos. Then you've got some pimps out here mistaking other pimps for *their* hos. Then you've got some dumb hos out here trying to ho for another ho, who ain't even interested in pimpin' his or her sorry behind in the first place.

The shit is a mess, I tell you. But it's beautiful too. It's beautiful and it's a mess. **Because it's all life baby.** "Life is a pimp's canvas. And a ho is the artistry he or she must handle." (Now that's another famous quote right there that I just came up with).

So let us not flee from this rich, gooey, funky, nasty, luscious, tasty, sickening thickness we have somehow cosmically backed up and spun around into. **Let us all just "put a mo' deeper flow into our ho, and try and pimp a little slicker, as the plot get's thicker."** One love baby!

Chapter VI

George Washington, the pimp-daddy of our nation
and Lady Liberty, once again,
hoin' for dollas.

Chapter VI

Stand Up, No Matter What!

"When you tell the truth, you are free simply by virtue of describing what is so. This descriptive language evokes a feeling of affirmation, a willingness to be, an appreciation for being alive in the world as it is. When someone speaks the truth, everyone around them is touched and there is hardly anything to say back except, 'Ain't it the truth?'"

Brad Blanton, Ph.D - "Radical Honesty"

Pimpaphobia- Fear of puttin' it down.

At this point, there is no use continuing to be inauthentic **all the time.** Suffice to say that if you have been consistently hoing up until this point, we can safely project that in the future, you will probably continue to ho. I think we've at least somewhat established that long-term hodom (or ho-hum) can also be viewed as a domain of possibility.

I know I can say that I personally have not really had any great success acting very pimpish when in fact somewhere down inside, in my heart of hearts, I knew that I was being a ho. And I am not worried in the slightest about sharing that with you because I am intimately familiar with this reality we call "human being." And almost everyone who hos periodically learns to appear as pimpish as they can, as much of the time as they can. So hey it's all cool with me. Try and fake it till you make it if that's what works out for you in the riddle.

But then there are you pimps, ever digesting your last tasteful meal of life. You have been the chosen ones to receive the coveted faculty of pimptation, that great enigma, that elusive long-lost birthright for so many. You are only here or there or anywhere for that matter, because of some chunk of prey that was somehow left untapped after your last swoop, your last inevitable conquest.

But yet you also, at times, hide and even suffer inside. You may even recall way back to a time when you too hoed. And it was very, very hard for you, because you may have had other family members or friends who were out there hoing along side you. But in spite of all the tough times, and all the struggle, and all the memories of really being pimped rather harshly at one point, you somehow still remember a lot of the good times....those wonderful rare spaces that all the big time pimping in the world can't duplicate.

And you remember how even though everyone struggled, they also supported and gave each other a lot of love. Yes, you truly did at one time, "love them hos." And they loved your ho ass in return.

But now, you note that things have changed. People look up to you, and admire your ability to pimp so tough. Some would give whatever they could to just be able to put it down as hard as you do. And yet there doesn't seem to be the same kind of love available, the same deep camaraderie that existed back in the day. Sure, you may pull up on the scene and instantly fade everybody with your display of power and prowess, and with all your "bling bling." But truthfully, you really do miss that deep ho love.

Unfortunately, the case so often times is that as long as you're out there struggling like a ho, no one's really mad at you, or being that resentful towards you. Why should they be? You're just the next can waiting for someone to come along and kick it. But now that you're the big pimp you always wanted to be, you are discovering that pimp-hate is of a plentiful supply, and available in varyingly subtle quantities.

Still you do not have, nor do you seek, a shoulder to cry on. You can't help it if you were born to pimp, anymore than certain people who have arrived in this dimension essentially to ho. Pimping is not only your fate, it is your "dreaming."

You would probably have to study more aboriginal philosophy to really grasp what I mean by "dreaming." But for now, if you find yourself reading this and going "Yeah, exactly. Pimping is my dreaming personality," then this is all probably somewhat true of yourself.

And all I'm saying is whether you are anywhere from the pimpinest of pimps to the hoiest of hos, the request is simply to stand up, and be counted. I don't mean in the numeric sense, I mean in the authentic sense.

Let's quit hiding from each other! Because we have all participated together in one way or another, in creating this dream- this bizarre, awesome, paradox-laden field of vibration we call everyday life. *And if you think it's very weird, it's because it's supposed to be that way.*

Just look at it. Look real deep, and move as you're viewing. Because that's how the universe is looking back at your bizarre human ass! The earth is spinning *right this moment* faster than the fastest pimp can pimp a ho. Faster than the fastest ho can.... well I guess faster than she can just be out there hoing real fast. But you get my point.

The world is looking back at you from a constantly moving, dynamic, fluxual point of viewing. Not a stagnant stationary one, homey. I should more accurately say *points* of viewing. For we are being viewed at this moment from a billion different viewpoints, that will all shift the next moment. Now who's ultimately pimping who?

Look, I told you it's all a riddle. And you can go check with a physicist who keeps current if you want to hear the most bizarre intellectual pimping conversation you've ever been either bored to death or fascinated by (depending upon your background).

How in the hell do you think we can have a conversation about this dream we call "freedom," in our modern world, and there are no pimps and hos present? It cannot possibly happen. *You have to have someone to pimp and someone to ho in order for there to be the freedom to either pimp or ho!* You can't just say "Okay, we've got rid of all them trifling ass hos, and now we're in the process of running all these over-posturing ass pimps off, so now we can all have freedom." No, uh uh. It won't work. *The pimping and hoing is what creates the freedom.*

I know it's strange, but that's the Tao. Light arises from darkness. Constriction causes expansion. The inner is produced by the outer. And the meaning of "cold" is created by the existence of "hotness." If there were no hot, then everything would be cold. And being cold would therefore lose its significance, its distinction. If you bought a new car, then how could I say, "Hey, that's a cold-ass ride you got there bro." It wouldn't be anything but another ride. It's only because of the existence of all the broken down, raggedy ass rides out there, that I can say that you have a "cold ass" ride, and it means something.

In other words, every element of life's bizarreness is necessary. If anyone has convinced you otherwise, then don't trip. You're certainly not the first ho on the earth to be pimped. And believe me, ***you won't be the last!!!***

You see, because dig this – it's not that we've got too much pimping and hoing going around. It's that we've got too much pimping and *hiding!* We've got too many people out here just psyched out of fully doing their thing in this whole dream.

You've got all kinds of pimps out here who are pimping so tough, they ain't even got time to look around and see how pimped up they are themselves. ***So they just can't fully come out and pimp,*** because there's too much bizarre shit out here going down! And it's all out of everyone's control.

Again, look at all these fools in Washington. Some of them are truly working hard trying to change things for the better, and some of them are just out there voting and vetoing shit like a poker game with the boys on Tuesday night in their mama's basement. Hell, if they were to be honest with your everyday-hard-laboring-ho-ass, they would just come straight out and tell you, "I don't know what's going on with over half this congressional bullshit, and I don't care. ***Because I'm going to get paid anyway!"*** All they know is that white people have to

Will the Real Pimps and Hos Please Stand Up!

basically hang together, and ride this shit out, like Martin Lawrence said, "Until the wheels fall off!"

Now however you can weave that into your benevolent American dream story, you weave it! Because it will not, I repeat, **will not get less bizarre,** thank you. As a matter of fact, thank yourself this time.

Because for a minute, all of this had me fooled. I was pimped up real tough in some red, white and blue Tommy Hilfiger sweats (brothers pronounce it "Hilfiga") and saying, "Hey, this is cool. From sea to shining sea, you know? I'm going to get me some pie. A nice tasty little slice."

But then I looked around at what was and is still happening in the world, and I thought, "Hey, America is doing this? They didn't talk about it on the six o'clock news. That's a twist." And then I looked around again and thought, "Here's another twist, and another." And pretty soon they had my black ass so twisted, I had to just pull up and do some real inner and outer researching.

And while it's only *a* point of view, I can share with you my own sense that no matter how thick the plot gets, and how twisted it is, it's all somehow appropriate. It's all appropriate in it's wildest, most diverse sense.

And that includes you and me. Like I said, it's okay that someone fooled us about ourselves. Because ultimately, they were just players in this great dreamed up game. And they played out whatever script they were handed, and made whatever modifications in it that they were able to, given what the script allowed them to see and be present to.

But in the end, you and me, well, we are the dreamers of this dream. ***However, it is only once in a great while on average that we loosen up and experience a moment*** *of that strange lucid recollection.* That you pimp and I ho, or I pimp while you ho, or we both pimp simultaneously, or ho synchronistically, or whatever, is just all part of this infinitely incredible storied fabric that our oldest ancestors called "the dreaming."

Now you won't find anything about it in your standard scholastic textbook. Aboriginal philosophy has been long since buried in our contemporary urban world, with the exception of only a couple of sources who'll remain well hidden in the woodwork.

We Americans are pretty much only aware of our own modern dreaming. We only look out at the cosmos through a web of definition and distinction woven by pimps in the scientific world, past and present, who have served the most politically powerful institutions of their era.

At this point, your perception has been so colonized, you don't have much of a chance of viewing yourself as anything other than a conventionally agreed upon, socially mechanized, consumer, buck chasing, run of the mill, twenty-first century urban grid fixture. So I'm making about as much sense to you talking about some aboriginal "dreamtime" concept as Dan Quale campaigning at a Taliban reunion! (And to think, his dumb ass might actually show up there).

The point is, about all you've got left besides a struggling local yogi, a sack of overpriced sage, and maybe some old Chopra video, is **your own raw, unprocessed authenticity, creativity and sense of humor to really empower you.**

So what if you just come on out and declare that you're pimping, or at least acknowledge a few other pimps publicly? So what if you just came back from hoing out there somewhere, started reading through this strangely intriguing book, and decided to somehow be more confident and open about who you are? So damn what!?

I mean, what do you think is going to happen in this dream? People are going to trip out if you just stand up? I got news for you baby, ***they're already tripping!*** They're already running around here like a chicken-eating ho with her head pimp slapped off!

You're the one that's all tiptoeing out here half the time. Tiptoeing through America's tulips! Tiptoe through the big pimp's garden. Why it's just like you're in some kind of fairy tale. You're all "Shhhh, don't wake the big pimp," because you know he's gonna wake up and probably pimp slap your silly ass all the way down the freakin ho-stalk!

I mean come on people. We human beings are just ridiculous. And I'm obviously no exception. These western pimps have got us all psyched out. We're running around here like Dorothy.

Now I know you know Dorothy. She was all twisted up in this joint called "Oz." If she were here today, she would surely say, "No I'm not interested in Oz anymore," because now it's a freakin' prison on HBO. Why even the wizard couldn't help poor Dorothy if that cast got to her. Now she might be interested in doing another deal with HBO. Maybe a guest spot on "Sex in the City."

But anyway we're running around here now like she was back in the day. Remember she had to find this great pimp they called "the wizard." You do recall that the wizard was a pimp, so this is the perfect tale to illustrate some crazy, yet substantive point I'm going to make.

Yes, the wizard was the biggest pimp known in all of Oz. And of course, the wicked witch was also putting down crazy game on all of these people. She had them running around like some scared little munchkin hos on amphetamines.

They're like the townspeople in America, except they really didn't have a ghetto. The ghetto wouldn't have worked out in that original plot though. Because if there had been some black ghetto munchkins, they would have interrupted all Dorothy's scenes, just talking loud and carrying on the way we do. And if they would have had some Mexican munchkins, there would have been too many of them, probably cutting that fake ass grass or whatever they could do to get on the payroll.

So the writers were smart. They just wrote us out. Instead they had Dorothy running around with this scarecrow (who was truly a dumb ho), this lion, (who was the most cowardly hoinest lion you ever saw), and a doggone tin man, who couldn't even qualify to be a ho because he didn't have a heart. You've got to at least have a heart to be a ho. What the hell would he be, a "tin-ho"?

Anyway, this bizarre foursome was running all around Oz or wherever, trying to find this pimp-ass wizard, so he could help them. Meanwhile they didn't even know that this supposedly big bad pimpin' ass wizard was really just this little old dude who was putting down plenty game on everybody!

Well, to make a long story short and get to the point, these supposedly big, invincible ass pimps around here in America will have you played right out of the game, running around every which-a-way, until you drop *trying to find the answer that you already are!*

And most of us don't even get paid for the brilliant act we put on all of our lives. We don't get paid for just falling in line with everything, agreeing to every convention and hiding under every popular customary freaking impulse or procedure.

We don't get paid for being suckered into being "normal." *So we only end up more inauthentic and ho-like.* And by the time you figure out this great cosmic game, if ever, you're so deeply entangled, you end up spending most of the time trying to back-strategize your way out of all the situations that you've unconsciously layered around yourself from the freakin' outset. And even that whole process may be occurring for you without you ever being present to it.

It's because we've stuck so many layers of stagnant emotional plaster and hyper-conventional texture coat over our original human experience, that now we've got to just keep full on nudging, shaking and gulping down hot cupfuls of transformational dialogue until we can again detect a pulse.

Other than that you can continue to walk around with a subliminal stick up your ass, probably implanted early on by the most influential group of psycho-political-theological magicians who rode through your community with a grant from the powers that be.

And I would like to send this message to you all in the most loving vibrational envelope that my heart can paste a quick stamp on, because I've got other things to do, just like you! So since we're now hopefully at least standing, *how 'bout we keep it moving.* Yes, let's keep it moving right on through ho.

Moving Through Ho

Ho, as we have established, is a distinct reality. When you are in this existential space of being, or dealing with someone who is in it, you can often attest to how real it is, depending upon your degree of presence. A ho, ho-ness, or shall we say "ho-mind," produces a vibrational frequency.

Because your thoughts and actions within this frequency are totally influenced by it, we can refer to this phenomena as the "ho-mind-field." Two or more hos can create a "group ho-mind-field." Now while ho-mind-fields may be very small or quite large, they do not have specific geographical boundaries. (You may refer to Mindell on group fields, but not on hos).

Yet a ho-mind-field will usually create a viewable effect upon the psychic and bodily activity of the person in it. On an individual level, you would note that the person displays certain distinct "ho qualities." For instance, you might interpret that a person does not think on a very autonomously productive level, as evidenced by his or her acquiescing conversational drawl, or somewhat suspended, "blank" facial expression. Now obviously interpretations maybe subject to error. The person may be either a rare pimp genius, who merely operates with a sort of "airy" appearance, or this may be a very slick pimp-centered individual who uses diversional social strategies.

But such cases are more the exception than the rule. Most hos are usually quite distinguishable. They simply aren't the ones putting down the game. They're the ones subserviently operating in the pimps plan, program or social scheme.

From looking at the surface you would probably guess that it's just a momentary choosing that has a ho actually being a ho. But the majority of the time, with most hos, you'll notice an on-going behavioral patterning. This patterning is caused by the frequency of the ho-mind-field.

If we use the model of a radio for instance, we note that it is constructed to receive or "pick up" certain signals. Radio stations have powerful transmitters that send signals at particular frequencies. The numbers on a radio dial represent the settings at which a radio can pick up certain signal frequencies. All of the stations together represent a collection of settings, which can receive a whole range of frequencies.

Anyway, I say all that to illustrate that the ho-mind-field is constituted by a certain range of frequencies which hos "pick up" like a radio. Pimps operate outside of these frequencies, these vibrations. Hos operate within them and therefore exist within a "ho mind state." ***Basically all day long, they pick up continuous "ho chatter."*** It's like a bunch of ultimately meaningless distraction and bullshit that passes for substantive thought or intelligent conversation. Too much of it can drive the average pimp crazy!

If you don't believe me, just think about someone who you know is a ho. I'm talking about one who you know for sure is just a consistently patterned ho. Now we'll apply this theory or theorem (or whatever the hell it is) to them.

Just reflect silently about this person for a moment without judgment or conversation. Reflect as if you are simply "picking up" whatever there is available at the moment for you to pick up about them. Now remember, be non-judgmental, for the person may also be reflecting about you right now, by some far out coincidence. (Wouldn't that shit be a trip?)

But now just reflect and see if you are getting that this person is usually such a patterned ho, because he or she only picks up the frequencies of the ho-mind, and therefore thinks, acts, walks and talks in the ho-mind-state.

You see all of this shit is crazy, yet there's quite a certain validity to it. You may be sitting up laughing, *but people are actually out there hoing, stuck in the frequency of the ho-mind-field, and they can't get out!* The closer they are to you, the more you may laugh *and* cry simultaneously.

For the ho-mind-field is insidious. It is universal. It does not discriminate, period. You've got U.S. hos, Canadian hos, French hos, Iranian hos, Czech hos, Australian hos, South African hos, Brazilian hos (some say they're the finest!), and Mexican hos. In fact a ho-mind-field could be global, but we don't have time to really focus on that. There's enough domestic hos to have us utterly drained right now.

And I do mean drained. Because someone has to think for all these hos! They certainly don't think for themselves. I mean they can add two and two, pick up the groceries, change the spark plugs, and work steady jobs (the majority of hos work real steady). Or hell, you can fill up a factory with them and it will run efficiently. But only so long as there's a pimp or two to put down and direct the game plan.

So you get what I mean. Pimps view the hos of the world as an ongoing management challenge that can become quite draining if it gets out of hand.

Will the Real Pimps and Hos Please Stand Up!

Now just because you identify somewhat with the pimp archetype, it doesn't mean that you can afford to become careless and not be present. For the ho-mind-field is very tricky, indeed. You might slip and cross over into it, and easily not be aware that you have.

Because we are dealing with the nature of frequency, and not a phenomena we can see, we are all basically susceptible. It may take days, even months for the average one of us to realize that we have been unexpectedly operating in the ho-mind-field. You could look up one day and suddenly realize that you have been lulled into just mindlessly putting in lots of hours, or even years on some job that doesn't really fulfill you, and moving along through your life like an outdated old machine. Perhaps you're like most when you have sort of gone to sleep in the tide of it all and your automatic "ho-pilot" has taken over.

You know the pounding pimp pace of our society will do that to you. That's why people call it the "rat race." They've got you scrambling like a rat through this bizarre insane pimp-constructed maze. And you're "racing." Which is really a kicker, because you're inner and outer human make up is not cosmically designed for being pounded constantly like a small lawnmower engine. Now how many people do you know with old broken-ass lawnmowers sitting up in their garages? Come to the hood, you'll find a whole gang of 'em!

So no wonder so many of us just slip into automatic ho-pilot. It's basically a form of defense mechanism. *Because many hos just straight up sense that they cannot hang with these pimpin' ass Americans out here.* Maybe they've attempted to pick up pimp frequencies and the signals just seemed too complex, or harsh on their psychic receivers.

The cold reality is some have conceded to just try and find a good pimp, or pimp group, and be as faithful and supportive a ho as they possible can. And what can you say? Ho-mind is hardly a place without possibility. So again, let's not mistwist on top of the real twist.

I'm just pointing out that the ho-mind-field exists, and that people may arrive in it from various different circumstances. It's just part of life for some of us. But just because you are in ho-mind, it doesn't mean you will inevitably end up in a *permanent state of "stagnant-ho-mindedness."* For *stagnant-ho-mind* is just a mere result, another existential place you may end up if you continually ho.

However, the stagnant-ho-mind is what you want to avoid, if at all possible. Stagnant-ho-mind takes place when the ho-mind-field becomes so subtlety and thoroughly overpowering that you just become a broke down or seemingly immobile ho. Not that you are necessarily immobile in a geographical sense, though this may also be the case. But you become so damn lethargic about your own initiative in life. Stagnant-ho-mind will leave your ass in the condition of an old shell of what you could possibly be.

And it's like quick sand! If you sense you're entering into it, you're like "Help! Please come pick me up!" Because you know you need to get to someplace where there's some kind of energy and aliveness. You don't hardly want to be left alone in stagnant-ho-mind if you've got any sense left. For the effects could be permanent. And *permanent stagnant-ho-mind* is like a helpless abyss between short-term stagnant-ho-mind and death. This is where heavily suffering addicts and depressive syndrome endurers end up. This is where not necessarily welfare recipients, but "welfare thinkers" end up. (By "welfare thinking/dreaming" I am referring to a condition that can exist regardless of whether one is on welfare or not).

You can go to almost any ghetto in the world and you will find the effects of a stagnant-ho-mind-field. You can literally feel or experience it all the way down in your bones. In some of the worse ghettos it's like being in the energetic field of a living graveyard. You feel how the most powerful and ruthless pimps of the world have just left this ho-mind-field "pimped to the bone." In most cases, the stagnant-ho-mind frequencies act upon the human psychic makeup like a vacuum, which slowly and sometimes totally reverses empowerment. Such experiencers are often unable to pick up any pimp frequencies whatsoever.

Stagnant-ho-mind also indicates that the ho-mind-field frequencies have become metabolized by the body. And this is why it is such a deep thing. *Because your dreams can only happen through you when you are able to fully metabolize them.* That is the only time your "acting" body is fully involved. In stagnant-ho-mind the only thing you will be putting down is your own tired ass!

So while Christian people say, "an idle mind is the devil's workshop," here we will maintain, "a stagnant mind is the common hos workshop." And believe you-me, they've got some hos out here who are working in the shop 'round the clock!

The reality is that in many ways, the human mind is pre-dispositioned to generally ho. Just try listening in on any two women, or two men, or any mixed combination for that matter, of people when they are engaged in gossip. Now you talk about some ho chatter! Yet it either drives you away, *or it infects you, and you join in.*

Many spiritual teachings emphasize staying away from gossip as a general rule. Strangely enough though, if you catch many of the same teachers on a relaxed night off, they're right out in the thick of it, picking up on every bit of "chat scrap" they can, on anybody and their mama. Certain kinds of ho chatter even creates a "stickiness" in the ho-mind-field frequency, and thus you end up stuck!

And that's why you need to know some pimps, no matter who you are. I don't care whether it's family, a friend, a lover, your boss, neighbor or whatever. You need a pimp in your life, period! Because a pimp who's down for you, will agitate you. He or she will agitate you not in a subtractive way, but in a constructive way. A pimp in your life will keep you awake and alert about making shit happen!

A pimp who's really down for you will not only keep mashing his or herself, but will piss you off periodically in a strategic way, just to bring you present to how much of a ho you keep being. He/she will let you know that all of these consistent ho-choices you make really don't serve you. They only encircle and entangle you further.

Because a pimp knows his/her role is to agitate a ho, anyway. I mean most pimps are friendly at a certain level, and so they have ho friends. They know that they just can't hang around pimps all the time, because a pimp that hangs around all pimps has to look out of the corner of his eye too much. Most of the time, that's just the nature of the game.

But the pimp, of course, knows that hos must continually be agitated at least somewhat, just so they can stay present to the game going on around them.

Because the pimp is going to continually comment on it. That's the way they are, period. For instance, if you took a ho into a empty room and asked "what do you see?" she/he would say, "I see merely an empty room." If you ask the pimp the same question, she/he would say, "I see a space in which this could happen, or someone is going to probably do such and such with this."

The pimp "sees" the game, or just *game,* because he picks up on the frequency of it. So a ho is always better off with a pimp in her/his corner, because let's face it, *hos are like bats - they cannot see!* (The game that is). So at least every once in a while, a ho needs help from a "seeing eye" pimp!

Dynamic Ho-Mind

At last, *for a ho who is authentic,* there is the possibility of moving into a positive space of his or her dimensionality that we can call the **dynamic ho-mind.** The dynamic-ho-mind is of course the opposite of the stagnant-ho-mind. And it is at the complete other end of the spectrum from the permanent stagnant-ho-mind! In the dynamic ho mind, the ho is clear about his/her honess, yet she/he has also attained a certain fluidity through this presence or knowledge.

Such a quality of presence is brought about by a) authenticity – the ho knows she/he is a ho and will stand erect and state that it is so (even if it's only at home in the mirror, one of the best places to start) b) the "seeing eye" pimp - the dynamic ho creates and maintains constructive creative relationships with pimps c) willingness - when the ho becomes a learner of what she/he can, and moves out of stagnancy, she is then creating a way of fluid opening and transformation. The universe then assists her/him in many ways, which were never thought possible. In fact, it is said that "when the ho is ready, the pimping teacher appears." d) nature herself - the natural flow of the cosmos is from yin to yang, and back in a continuous cycle. It is an endless creative, evolving dance. Once the ho has entered the state of dynamic ho mind, she/he has also become once again a magically dimensional being, a transformer. Therefore, the ho you are looking at one moment, may become the pimp you are looking at the next!

Moving Into Pimp

Like ho, you want to move through pimp as well. But you don't want to move *away* from pimp. No siree. I would say that what would be best for anyone is to understand as much as they can about the nature of "pimp mind." And this will enable them to use and create it as a powerfully unique experience that will serve them in the greatest fashion. Because I'm sorry if you haven't gotten this point up until this far, but to be straight up honest, *the pimp is the essence, baby!*

It doesn't have anything to do with who shot John, or who was an everlasting scumbag. For the days of the original cultural expression and pathways of pimping are now transforming. Sure, people still walk the streets at night, and even operate in high-class luxury establishments. But pimping as a whole has forever expanded, and in many cases "shape shifted."

The old original form of pimping will still remain and be respected in the street context, and even in some of its classier settings. But more and more, as evolution pushes forward, they will begin to be viewed somewhat like dinosaurs. (We'll call 'em Pimp-o-saurs.)

However, a basic pimp in today's swiftly evolving world may be viewed from several angles. He or she maybe interwoven with other pimps, with his/her hos, or with any number of freelance independent hos in a variety of economic, political and social contexts.

Because as many of you know already, hos just can't compete anymore. ***Our "freefall" into globalization has radically changed what it even means to be a human being.*** As a ho today, if you are not at least very dynamic, then you're probably scarcely if at all able to see yourself anywhere near a conversation about social empowerment. Modern pimping now exists to the extent that you are only viewed as a third or fourth-class citizen, at best.

The world is just not what it was twenty or thirty, or even ten years ago. It has become not "Planet of the Apes," but "Planet of the Pimps." I mean you see these people like Michael Jordan and Tiger, and Sean "P. Diddy" Combs (he makes sure you see his ass often in videos, magazines and anywhere else), and you hear about a Bill Gates, and you say to yourself, "Damn, these people are proving one thing – pimping is infinite! It's never ever, ever, going to stop!"

So if that's the case, you think to yourself, "Let me focus some more on this dynamic-pimp-mind stuff, that this crazy character 'E. Brown' or whoever is trying to tell me about." Because nowadays, pimp-mind is not to be taken lightly at all. You and your constituents have a lot at stake. You have big games going on in life, in which you must perennially maximize.

If you can go to a university and take a class on photography, or culinary development, or operating in a multi-lingual social environment to add to your education and expand your ability to go out in the world and make your dreams come about, how come you can't go take a specified course on pimping? Hell, they could dress it up and give it a fancy name like, "Developing Strategies for Pimpratory Acquisitions in Business," or "Pimpalogical Philosophy and Structural Implementation in the Twenty-First Century." I mean really, you don't care. All you want is for someone to show you how to develop *your* pimping. You want them to help you maximize, and unfold the pimp that is within you. The hell with walking up and down that damn campus seemingly forever, while you just get pimped further every time you do so much as stop at a cola machine.

I mean I'm just saying why can't we be real? Why can't America just be honest and say to the whole world, or the United Nations, or whoever in a very diplomatic manner, "We've noticed that there's been a great amount of change happening in our global dynamic. And in keeping with our competitive philosophical tradition, we will be phasing in a more advanced pimpratory curriculum at the national collegiate level," period.

Hey, you never know. The United Nations might be impressed. *They might ask, "How much will it cost for us to get some of that? As much doggone hoing as we've got going on up in here!" You know, they might say, "Go on and sell us the deluxe package!"* Because they know how rough its getting out here. I'm telling you and you may quote me, "What the world needs now is pimp, sweet pimp. It is the only thing that there's just not enough to go around, dammit!"

Moving into Active Pimp-Mind

It is important that you move into an *active pimp mind state.* You can dib-dab in and out of pimp mind, but things will not start to fully come into fruition for you until you significantly activate your *dynamic pimp-mind potential.* Other than that you will wastefully teeter-totter and end up right back you know where (Good! You remember).

Being a pimp is all about mashing, straight up. Pimps are utter completionists. They are consummate "see-it-through-ists" if you will (or if you won't, shit, we're talking about pimping). A ho may be buried up to his or her neck in incompletions, but a pimp builds upon completeness.

That is why they don't do well adhering to the rigidity of rules. For a pimp only sees the rules as the work of another pimp (or pimp group). So he or she's main focus is on creating reality and completing the particular phase of the game that is being put down. The rules only signify an adjustable feature on the landscape upon which the pimp creates.

The world of people is like a world of brushes or art supplies which the pimp uses to blend the main objects or objectives on his life canvas. In a profound way, to the pimp, it's all art. "Pimp-art," that is. It's all pimp-art and stupidity! For there are many other artists, but there is even more stupidity splattered everywhere. The pimp's commitment is to stay alert in the world of people, put down the game, and avoid as much stupidity as possible.

That's why if you notice, pimps are very confident. Because while a ho is occupied with doing basic affirmations and fluctuating in and out of doubt, or worry, the pimp skips past the whole "belief in oneself" conversation, and goes right on into step three or four of taking action. He or she does not muddle around in some ho-lack conversation. Thus we can refer to our goal as ***active pimp-mind.***

You know it when you are there. The most awesome athletes report being in an almost eerie sort of "zone." Everyone recalls watching Michael Jordan in many a last minute situation. It didn't matter whether you were rooting for him or not. You could see it in the faces of the opposing players. It didn't matter. Mike was in fully active pimp-mind. He would always complete the play on your ass. And then he would come back the next year and complete the next.

Because the thing about this active pimp-mind is that once you step into it, it expands. And as it expands, you expand. You expand right into this whole strange dreaming process that life is. For instance, right now I am writing my behind off trying to finish this project, and it's almost finished. But by the time you read it, expansion baby! So fortunately at this moment, I am in active pimp-mind, or to be more precise, the ***active pimp-mind mode.***

A ho, conversely, is often experiencing some miscellaneous form of contraction. The universe is not really expanding for most hos. Rather it expands around them. ***It expands everywhere, but where the ho is standing!*** And this is only shifted by the ho standing near any accessible pimp.

Will the Real Pimps and Hos Please Stand Up!

Right now, as I'm writing, George Bush and a bunch of other crusty numbskulled pimps in Washington are focusing in on a *crusty numbskulled pimp mastermind plan,* to expand in the middle east, believe you-me. The code phrase for the whole fiasco is probably "operation crusty!"

Now they're not asking anyone "Should we be there?" No siree. They're just going to go there and put it down whether the American people or the whole world say whatever. Because they don't care if you ideologically support them or not in this. All that's surface conversation. Whether you march til' your big toe starts to stick out and you say, "Hey, I'm starting to get cold. Better pack it up for the day, and hit it back early tomorrow," they don't care. *Because they're going to go over there anyway, helllloooooooooooo!*

Even if they tell our gullible ho-asses they're not going over there, they're still going to go. As a matter of fact, they're there, again, as we ho (I mean speak). They're there right now, bombing shit up, pimp-slapping Sadam's soldiers, and taking their oil. The trouble with these degenerate ass pimps that run the government is, they carelessly maim and demolish too many innocent civilians. And then they tell your gullible ass on the news, "Job well done." And you go back to the factory.

But if you're able to move into active pimp-mind mode, then all this becomes plain. It's just more artistry. More pimp-art. And then of course there's the non-pimps stupidity, which consist of reactionary conjecture, and intensified ho-mind-field chatter. And none of this means anything more to the pimp than the "dust" on the furniture of his or her program. That's all the ho's thoughts amount to- "ho-dust."

And this is the cold dusty truth to be told. For I am certainly in active pimp-mind mode at this moment, as you might have guessed. *And in such a mode, as many of you already know, you exist as an ultimately "spoken" individual.*

The Bundle of Expression

What I mean by "spoken," could be thought of in the following way. We all come into the world in a little bundle. Let's call it a bundle of nerves or "luminous fibers." And this little bundle that we come into the world as, is like a perceptual *supersponge.*

Now the supersponge that we start off as, does not have a developed faculty of speech. The supersponge only has the initial ability to absorb the styles of creating reality, or "dreaming" with speech, that the larger, older bundles have spun.

Yet if the larger, "older bundles," or adults, do not have a style of creating reality with speech (dreaming) that allows them to express that *this is exactly what is taking place,* then how could they be skillfully honest in communication in many other crucial areas of relating to themselves or the other supersponges? After all, it's a little hard to be rawly honest and put it down, when you don't even grasp the nature of the matrix that we live in. Some part of the conversation will inevitably be missing.

Perhaps you can see how not being able to follow our own conscious and unconscious processes (the cosmic game) leaves adult humans impaired as communicators? Because of course who is sponging all of this, but the little supersponges we all originally start off as? ***We are in fact, continually recycling a great deal of our own unconsciousness.***

And where I'm going with this is that we are simply not skilled at being honest and following ourselves, because we are too busy following the perceptual "rules" we were taught by millions of other people, who are simply not skilled at being honest and following themselves either. ***In other words, we are born into a herd of inauthenticity.***

It's sort of like a great cosmic trick. Because if you are inauthentic, or unable to just follow yourself and be rawly honest about what you discover, then you will eventually be tripped up by this habit when it comes to using speech. ***You will not be "spoken," because you will be too busy trying to follow some inauthentic ass "reality game," rather than creating the more authentic one you have the innate capacity to.***

You will either end up ***underspoken*** from all the inhibition that has built up and been sponged up layer by layer, as you've continually become more confused about who should be responsible for spinning whose reality. And in this, like most of us, you will be conditioned to create only a mere survival-based dream, or some half-ass "brownie" acceptance points. Or at best, you may receive a well-nestled reward for being a brilliant "yes person" in the system.

Or you will become often too outspoken, meaning that you have the ability to express yourself, but you easily and unskillfully wear out your welcome in the ongoing group process. You may end up having to develop more of a sense of rhythm in communication in order to weave with and into our collective dreaming, rather than out of a powerful connection with it. For if you consider that there aren't any born hermits out here, *you'll only acknowledge and capitulate to the fact that your nature to dream is a communal one. We are all inherently committed to one another at some authentic level of being.*

Yes, the truth is that being "spoken" is quite a feat for the developing sponge. It is both a rare skill and an art. Because you must honor and live up to your total paradox, your divine, beriddled, human juxtaposition. For you are obviously the individual, who is as contoured, unique, primped and self-glorified as many a proud moment calls forth. And no one fails to dance in their own individuality, particularly in western dreaming. In the east, this dance can be ultra subtle in some groups. Yet the fact that we speak at all means being "spoken," or *fully self-expressed* is an ultimately irrepressible topic.

But while all this individuality is taking place you must also explore, discover, honor and come to grips with your "group self," your innate communal beingness. *Because here is where you must ultimately take your seat (or any seat for that matter), on our collective human merry-go-round.* And this will certainly be the scariest, most bizarre merry-go-round you'll ever ride at certain points. But it will also be that cosmic ride from which all of the rides are possible.

Being the group that you are means that you can't just keep getting pissed off and walking out of our group dreaming because it irks, frustrates, manipulates, misleads and confuses you so at any given moment. *From the point of view of your group identity, it is you who is both the creator and the participant of such experience.* In other words, *you are the group.* You are irking, frustrating, manipulating, misleading and confusing yourself inside of your own collective dream, buddy. According to Mindell, this is how you unconsciously evolve, awaken and "dream yourself up"- through a mysteriously, self-agitating path.

And in this sense you are quite an evolving, dancing, and complexly interwoven, human puzzle. *So you find in dealing with yourself, or "yourselves" for that matter, that it may not always be possible to please both your individual and group self at the same time.* You might often run into conflict between the two aspects. And yet you are still in the midst of all this process continuing to dream and create your reality through speech, while being either authentic and open, or inauthentic and misleading to yourself and others.

And as if the plot is not thick enough, the game becomes even more challenging. Because as an individual, you basically want and choose to go for the "gusto" (even if you don't drink beer), meaning you want to create as great a life experience as you can, as powerfully as you can. *But group rules and social protocols are full of riddles.*

Groups are not always honest, nor do they seem interested in honesty when it comes to certain issues. So you will in turn become led into this sort of strange psychological burial ground, where social and personal truths that are repressed may never be dug up and *expressed.* And this in turn becomes your everyday given socio-political obstacle course of inauthenticity. *And to top it all off the pressure continues to mount for you to conform and minimize your "boat rocking" capacity.* For you have been offered enough, the group will argue. Now you must somehow make it all work.

The answer to being cosmically stuck between such a rock and a hard riddle? Simple... pimp! Pimp your way right through it all! For the pimp in you most certainly has a perspective that will put all else into perspective. The pimp cuts through all the internal hesitancy and goes straight for the "promised" zone, which is the everyday world just as it is – an abundant pimping ground.

Pimps aren't really hung up in society's problems. They are choosier, and wiser than to get all hung up in the "hang-you-up-trips" of other pimps. And they surely aren't hung up with the hang-ups of any hos!

This enables the pimp to be "spoken" without being over-powered by the draining conflicts of the world. He knows his status entitles him to bold, unentangled honesty. And this is hardly to imply that all of them are honest. Yet the pimp is not the tongue biter by far. A ho may have to gnaw that tongue like a stick of gum sometimes, but not the pimp. After all he notes, the description of the world, as we know it, is created by his own kind.

The Scholastic Gameboard

In school, we learn of a pimp named Columbus who "discovered" America. Now the natives that were already here long before he arrived have received no credit for any such "discovery." I guess because they were already here in the first place. Obviously this place didn't exist until the white guy said so.

In math and science, we learn about Isaac "the Appleman" Newton, who probably was hanging out around some "pippin" apple tree when he founded his first theoretical ho, or ho-theory- that apples fall downward, like everything else. And of course he fully elaborated on that, or we wouldn't know of his pimpin' ass today. I guess we'd be thinking the apples fall up!

We also have our modern "grid" from philosopher Rene Descartes, who basically said "if anything or any ho out there doesn't show up on my pimp grid where I can measure and keep an eye on it, then it flat out doesn't exist. *So he and his scientific cohorts are responsible for all these ultra-materialistic, superficial ass western hos running around here today.*

In psychology we learn of Freudian pimping. Or shall we say more accurately, Freudian pimping helped us see our own pimping. Why he gave the very western pimp-core its name – the "ego." So we really owe this brilliant, yet perverted cokehead a favor. Because we needed that name in order to be more focused on ourselves.

Without his contribution, westerners would be out here all off course. We would just be out here "trippin'," instead of out "ego tripping," like we really know how to do. Because you can see how we went right for the egoic root, and left the frill. No one's out there talking about someone's "id tripping," or saying, "you know, you've got a really big superego." It's not happening, because those parts of Freudian dreaming, or pimping, or whatever were not as useful to us. *They didn't strike the core of our own dreaming the way the ego concept did.* Just look at us. We're all like, "Ego…yeah, give us that!"

And that's why the west is a proud place for a pimp. The game is fast out here and you have to be fast to keep up with all the ways in which it's coming at you. *If you're truly up on your game, then you'll speak right into the face of this whole matrix as you go about your existence.* You'll be spoken, and you'll put it down as you have too.

Who knows? You may walk right into your school, or institution of higher learning, and say, "Hey professor so and so, I'm doing my thesis paper this year on pimping." Because you're feeling more and more like a true American. You may point out that those names and contributors in all the textbooks that you were required to read and memorize were certainly not just yielding to other people's ideas and concepts. You can remind your professor that he or she is also only dealing with those names because he/she had to, like everyone else. You can say, "I'm doing this paper sir/mam because like it or not, we all must deal with the pimp."

Visionary

You know, you have to be a true visionary, and at least somewhat of a pimp, to put it down when all the ears around you are totally unfamiliar with what you speak. Inventors are like this. In fact, inventors of possibility are often just like this. They act upon pimp-like impulses when they are defiantly creative. ***Their visions must agitate the convention or status quo, because they know the "world," or status quo usually needs a good shaking just to remember its truer self.***

Most of us tend to become entrapped in the subtle layers of the ho-mind from prolonged exposure to a state of usuality or "alwaysness." It's like once we become so evolutionally stagnated, even the universe itself just fills in whatever vacuum areas there are and pimps us. *It is sad, but so many of us humans spend a great deal of our lives just being pimped along by an old and outdated way of thinking.*

I remember seeing a concrete example of this when I read a book that contained an excerpt from a mainstream newspaper, printed a few years before Alexander Graham Bell invented the telephone and literally pimped the whole game (because I pay my telephone bill to S.B.C. every month!). The excerpt had a commentary by one of those know-it-all, opinionated-ass columnists. And in it, the columnist wrote that this "Bell guy" was a quack for talking about being able to talk to another human being over a wire in the near future. And I bet you anything that at the time, he had every sucka ass conventional intellect in town laughing, with their hard-headed, close-minded ho asses. Yet you know as soon as the first affordable phones came out, that columnist got one and was on it day and night just-a-fillin that line up with ho chatter!

So it's no surprise then that the modern day pimp scratches up the clarity of our ordinary viewing, and shakes up the stagnant groove in our ordinary doing. After all, in many cases these visions will greatly affect the group. So in a sense, they belong to more than just the individual having them. *The inventive pimp must therefore "bring it," in an agitative, yet consistently unstoppable way.* He/she can't wait for the ho to grasp what is going down, or "see the vision." If a ho could see beyond what there is in front of her/him, then she would become the pimp. But a pimp will hardly hold his or her breath two seconds waiting on that!

So he/she must be strategic. He must be patient and work the game with the proper sense of timing. There are probably some pimps reading this right now and saying to themselves, "you know dat's right!" Because they're straight up in the midst of putting down an ever more elaborate game, and they know that many of the hos around them wouldn't "see them," or what they're up to no matter how much they could try to explain. In fact, their trying to explain the game at some levels to the ho, would blind her/him even more than just keeping quiet about it. And that's the sad thing indeed, because I know some of you really, really feel me on that.

Because I too am a visionary, baby. *And I didn't write this book to miss my real everyday constituency, while pandering to some group who just will not understand no matter how much I bend over and try to make it more intellectual or "palatable."* So if you find yourself going, "I don't understand all this," then let's be real. You probably never will!

I mean I have certainly tried my damneddest to relate some of the perspectives from both sides of this dichotomy. But to be honest, I can't please all these hos out here. But what I can do, in a rather pimpish fashion (if I do say so myself), is convey the dynamics working behind and on top of all this *so we can perhaps get that in the broader context, it's all good! It's all appropriate anyway you wanna come.* And that's vision, baby boy!

Lucid Pimping

Well, we're now in the last of the home stretch (or possibly even the ho-stretch for some). And since we've covered so much and you're still reading (which is amazing in itself), I think it's about time for us to really just break it on down and shift into a less "outer" space, for a minute or two.

Because all of this has been both provocative, and kind of fun. And yet the average one of us still has great challenges to contend with right now, this minute, and in the future. We're still here in this increasing whirlwind within America's bodily and psychic landscape. I mean we can't just block it all out forever. So we've got to make it into what we want, into our own vision. We've got to attempt to pimp in a more lucid fashion.

Now many of you have been out there consistently on the front line pimping anyway, or at least pimping in spurts. But the game is tough. *And the key thing is that we've got to focus in on that which will give us greater focus.* Why that's it! We've got to focus on focusing, dammit! Before we try and focus on anything else, and run off like a blurry-eyed ho, we've got to slow down and deal with our focus. Some of us have a good system in place of folks who contribute to our game on a daily basis. And this is so important, when you can honestly say, "I have plenty of pimp support." It really makes it all so much more pleasurable.

But then there are those of us who day in and day out are trying to get down, and yet we are too often plagued by all this senseless ho-chatter. It's downright problematic walking around all day hearing these crazy ho-tapes playing in and out of the back of our minds. All down in our subconscious mind... and showing up in our interpersonal relationships. While we find out down the line that it was all as if we were reading off some stupid ho-script, implanted in us by society during childhood. All up at night having ho-mares, and even in the daytime. With all that going on, sometimes it's just a blessing to be at the job or at home, and be able to just chill and have a nice quiet moment of pimp for a change. No ho-chatter!

But again that's quite a feat in this day and age. ***Because however you do it, you must have a consistent approach that allows you to access your "inner pimp."*** Your inner pimp is like a light. Perhaps only a candlelight. But being in touch with it consistently will allow you to pimp the biggest game of your life!

Now many of you already have elaborate personal rituals by which you stay in touch with this light. For this pimp-light is your pimp right! But for some of you who are still of an open minded framework, the following exercise is offered;

An "Inner Pimp" Meditation

This particular meditation is for increasing one's focus by working with the breath, as well as using a helpful affirmation or two. Anyone can do it who is of a mature enough age to get a damn job! All you have to do to get started is sit in a quiet space, in a relaxed position where your spine is erect. Stretch your back, so that you do not hunch (hunchback pimps are very rare, so you don't want to narrow your chances). Now close your eyes, take three long, slow deep breaths, and then recite "Here goes nothing," as you re-open them. Then proceed further.

Focus upon your breath in conjunction with the idea of being an unequivocal pimp. *Allow yourself to breathe deeply with the sense that there are no apologies for doing what you've got to do, putting the game down, and making it all happen.* Envision yourself as a co-operator with the cosmos in creating whatever reality you wish (even if this comes out looking rather bizarre). Then, begin to gradually still the mind.

You'll probably notice a bit of ongoing "chatter." That's ho-chatter, and frequency residue that you've picked up from being out in the public ho-mind-field. Be still and just observe it in a detached way (maybe the shit will leave you alone!). But if it doesn't dissipate completely, then just leave it be. It can only stop you from connecting with your inner pimp if you continually focus on it.

Now imagine a light, about the size of a candlelight. Focus in on it. Breathe deeply, and feel the vibrancy of its flame.

Now don't be trippin' and laughing so much, or you'll blow the shit out by accident. Then you'll have to do a damn relighting meditation! But anyway, remain quiet and just be with the light. This light will give you the ability to pimp whatever you wish (as long as its fairly constructive), if you stay connected with it.

Now we're going to try one or more affirmations. *Pimp affirmations that is.* First, while still in a state of quiet focus, say to yourself these words;

I am a pimp. And I know this to be true deep down. *(Repeat one time)*

Then say:
I will put game down, **_regardless!_**
(Now repeat that shit three times, so it'll really soak in)

Next come back with:
I can pimp! (Five times just to drive the point home! And repeat it faster each time)

Oh yeah, this one is very essential to the whole process, for it brings it home on a unique personal level:
I alone create and define how pimping shows up for me.
(Say it only once, but with absolute conviction)

For you must understand that you will always be an absolutely unique expression of your own creative style of pimping. It cannot happen any other way, people.

Now we'll finish up with a little visualization. Just close your eyes, kick back and let your thoughts flow momentarily, while visualizing yourself in a place where the air is clean, the sun is shining and the landscape is vibrant and rich. Visualize this as a place where the pimping is good and plentiful year round. Where fresh, healthy (non-trifling) hos abound in great number. And you find them in both your interior and exterior landscape. They may just as well be your own viewing systems, efforts, skills or talents, as some outsider's. But whatever the case, the key is to visualize abundance. Visualize a beautiful, abundantly creative pimping ground.

If you have trouble visualizing fresh clean air, then don't fret. There can be great concentrations of hos found in smoggy urban areas for sure. It's definitely workable.

Now again, just breathe *into* this wonderful vision and hold it in a deep place within yourself, *and it will be manifested in some shape or form.* It may not be the exact form you saw in your vision or the one you thought you would manifest, but it'll be something, dammit!

As you come out of this deep meditation, open your eyes slowly. Now take three final deep breaths, look around you, and then go about your damn business! Because this pimp meditation/affirmation is very powerful and you have to give it time to soak in and take effect. Don't even go near any hos or talk about them for at least one hour after this exercise is finished. If you live with one or more, then leave for an hour or so. Go have a cup of coffee or tea or whatever you've got to do to separate yourself from them doggone hos for a minute.

I know it may sound crazy, and it is. But this exercise can be very effective. Some who have used it have reported dramatic shifts in their daily interactions with people. They report a new found sense of confidence, inspiration and just plain out *game* comes over them!

But you've got to be careful. This one fool did the meditation and went out and pimp-slapped three people in one day, including his boss! He ended up requiring some additional counseling. *You have to understand people, pimping is more profound these days. It ain't about going out there and being a damn fool.* Underestimating the power of connecting with the inner pimp can be dangerous.

On the other hand, if you complete this exercise and then you find yourself out there walking up and down Sunset Blvd, or having people still treat you any ol' kind of way, then perhaps you need to try doing it at least three times a day! And increase the affirmations to about 50 to

100 reps. Because yo shit is tow up! And you need to get down and do some serious inner and probably outer work too. But don't worry. Because whoever you are, you are certainly not alone!

End of the Line

Well folks, we're finally at the end of this rather raw, rhetorical sojourn. And I hope that if you have gotten anything from this reading experience, you may somehow be benefited by it. *I think we must admit that the truly full conversation of life requires more than just a tid-bit of gumption to undertake.* For whether we actually voice the full conversation or not, we all will in fact move through the actual bodily experience of every impactive reality around us. And who knows? *Maybe one day the universe, as an honest conversation, will actually be able to have itself.*

For there is definitely some deep shit going on around here. I mean just the other day I woke up feeling very tired and groggy. I had been up almost all night working on this manuscript. Suddenly a wild notion occurred to me. I thought, "Hmmm, I wonder if my soul is pimping my body, and using it as a linear time-space manifestational ho-vehicle!" Now that would explain why I was up all night. My soul wouldn't let me rest until I, in some sense, "stayed out on the street" and finished this book!

"Wow," I pondered. "This could possibly open up a whole new path of inquiry." But then I said to myself,

"Naw....that's too far-fetched. I must be just trippin' again."

In the meantime, like I said, I did not create the pimp and the ho. Nor did you. But I am also not here to side step the issues that occur for me. Life is just not about that, I believe. Life is about noticing, exploring, and being as real as you can, and as irrepressible as you can. And that's kind of what I notice that a pimp does. So I'll take that road.

As for my beloved hos, well, we've just got to realize that no matter what life looks like for us, we're just as much a part of the dream as anybody! And we're a little tired of getting our can kicked so much and always having our ho-backs up against the wall. Too bad we don't know how to really put anything down, or we'd probably form a national ho union. Or maybe even a global one.... and call it "Horon!"

You know, whatever you've got to do to just stand up and be about what you're about. That's the message. *And that's what I'm talking about.* In the mean, good peoples, I want to wish you...

A very, merry happy hoing.

And

A prosperous new pimping!

The End

Recommended Reading

"Stupid White Men" Michael Moore

"Addicted to War" Joel Andreas

"Radical Honesty" Brad Blanton

"Sitting in the Fire" Arnold Mindell

"Leader as a Martial Artist" Arnold Mindell

"Rich Dad, Poor Dad" Robert Kiyosaki

"The Lucid Dreamer" Malcolm Godwin

"Tao Te Ching" Lao Tzu

"Iceberg Slim" Donald Goines

"The Autobiography of Malcolm X" Alex Haley

"From Pimp Stick to Pulpit-It's Magic: The Life Story of Don 'Magic' Juan" Ann Bromfield, Don Juan, Katheryn L. Patterson

Recommended Viewing

"American Pimp"
"Superfly"
"The Mack"
"Pimps Up, Hos Down"
"Malcolm X"

Acknowledgements

Man, it's been all gravy....all gravy and some blissful, but hard ass work. But we, and I do mean we, pulled it off. These people just cranked and supported and listened to me run my mouth and bounce ideas around and did whatever miscellaneous crap it took. They are all heroic to me.

But first, it's always on point to stop and acknowledge the Creator, and the brilliantly creative, yet diverse oneness that the universe actually is.

Secondly, I must acknowledge and thank my parents for just "being" in such a way that it created the space for me to evolve, uniquely create and powerfully express myself. While I do not take it for granted, I will take it.

My daughter is the greatest living inspiration for me from day to day. If I share or ask her about something, she's gonna tell me straight how she sees it. Sometimes I have to check her because she's actually puttin' it down on Daddy so tough, she's got me scratchin' my head. Anyway I had to go on and officially put her on as a consultant for this project. A lot of kids are just sharp, so what else can you do but put 'em down?

My business partner and life companion, Zabrina Horton, has been no less than extra-extraordinary. But you could easily predict she would be that if you really knew her. She not only assisted in all the phases of this project, but she also spearheads the publicity and marketing with great zeal and timely strategy. This would probably be a raggedy ass effort without Zabrina, aka Agent Z.

My godfather Maurice Haws facilitates the whole overall apparatus being greased with a lot of wisdom. He keeps it very greasy, that's all I've got to say.

Keith Weathers and Love are my two best friends that wove right on into this whole book business conversation. They're both powerful listeners, and that's what enabled this vision to sustain like it has. I'll still have to create enough ways to truly thank them.

Tamisha Spencer not only helped me compile a lot of this craziness, but having the background she does, I really paid close attention to all of her feedback. Tank you, tank you, tank you baby.

Adam Pitt from the "Thriving Artists Group" (www.thrivingartists.org) hooked me up with this incredible illustrator, named Kajiah, and the gallery got rolling from there. It's all about the perpetuation of creativity in this life, so check out Thriving Artists, that's all I've got to say.

My man Jamal, aka "Mahli," has always had this very charismatic, real deal hood-boss type persona. He has heavily influenced me in my own sort of personal "pimp evolution." Sometimes I may even borrow his mannerisms, (consciously or unconsciously) when I'm puttin' it down just to insure greater impact. And he's preparing to drop a little somethin' down hard on all of us

– some of dat real dezzy. So much thanks to the whole crew at 60-40 Music.

To B. Lee; as long as you know how great your purpose is bra, take aim within yourself and it's on.

Lawrence Ebow, Rid, Fish, Sleepy and the whole crew at After Life Records are all keeping it poppin'. (Check out www.curbserver.com). It's like what else can a pimp do? They surely gets down wit E. Ray and that's something which I'm very proud to say. The love is definitely mutual, homies. Let's make this soundtrack happen!

Chapter One is making it all crack, once again. So much love to Greg, Drew and Brown for weaving it all up. Check out the website www.HipHopBodega.com.

And then there's Belma Johnson, the ultimate entrepreneurial pimp coach/consultant. His self-publishing course is a must for any and everyone. He's all about demystifying and disseminating pure game. (See www.belmaj.com).

Thanks goes out to Mr. Goldberg for the corporate coaching. I feel like a you-know-what in that world anyway. So I needed the "seeing eye."

Special thanks to Tami, Rashidi, Stacey and Cedra for the needed contribution and quick service. Also thanks go out to Akil from Jurassic 5, Ric aka Big Spicy, John and Leticia, Rico, Shorty, Shapavu, Fame, Afomia and Makeeta.

The Illustrators and Design Team

These pimpsters took some skill to recruit. But no where near the artistic skill they each possess on the canvass court. They were all excellent as you can see. Each made this whole creative adventure possible. So let's just break down the mad deep starting line-up.

At right guard, **Kajiah:** George Bush, Bill Clinton, Oprah Winfrey, Johnnie Cochran, Snoop Dogg, Bill Gates, Ice Cube, Tupac, Uncle Sam, George Washington and Lady Liberty.

At left guard, **Manny Avetisyan**: Denzel Washington, Samuel L. Jackson, P. Diddy, Malcolm X, Bush in front of the capitol building, E. Raymond Brown.

At forward, **Kevin Adams:** Don King.

At forward, **Chris Rinier:** American dreamer, Donald Trump, new pimp order pyramid, pimp gallery cover.

At front and center, my man **Xavier Savant:** Cover design and www.ghettophysics.com website.

Off the bench in the fourth quarter, bustin' long threes, **Harley Barrow, aka Pupa:** Bishop Don Magic Juan, Lil' Kim.

It was all love (and negotiation of course). The beautiful thing about it is that we are all from diverse ethnic backgrounds, but we came together under one outstanding common goal – creative pimpin' and making some dollas, dammit!

A Final Shout Out

A final shout out goes to a young brotha who I only knew for less than a year. But in the short time in which I crossed paths and worked with him, he was always a very strong, positive and totally supportive presence, a "demonstrator" in his own artistically definitive way. He was always very self-assured and driven, and in the midst of putting it down on the next level.

I last saw him a week before his life was cut short in some kind of utter riddle. We talked at the dinner table about this book. I remember very clearly how he graciously pledged his support and said "don't worry, it's goin' down." His name is Merlin Santana. Chill in peace, baby. As you can see, it's down.

About the Author
E. Raymond Brown

E. Raymond Brown is an African-American writer, musician, producer, technician, lecturer, workshop facilitator and full-time Daddy. He has studied geo-politics, pan-Africanism, somatic psychology, archetypal psychology, aboriginal psychology, Taoism, shamanism, metaphysics and quantum theory. Yet he has not one damn degree in any of them. So what! It certainly hasn't stopped him from puttin' it down. You're reading the book aren't you??

It's kinda like this guy had been pimped too hard for too long by this whole doggone American system. 'Til one day, he said the hell with it and put it all down.

Titles that You May See in the Future From E. Raymond Brown:

"Think and Grow Pimp"

"How This Ho Got Her/His Groove Back"

"Countering the Conspiracy to Destroy Young Black Pimps"

"Waiting to Exho"

"The Miseducation of the Pimp"

"As the Ho Turns"

"Chicken Soup for the Ho"

And always remember people, as my friend Love says, "Don't judge a pimp by his cover." Peace.

Email your comments, opinions and pimp perspectives to pimpadvisory@ghettophysics.com

And visit www.ghettophysics.com regularly for pimp updates.